RYAN NEWELL

Dark NLP

**Your Great Guide For NLP And Dark Psychology To
Understand The Art Of Using Your Mind To Become
The Master Of Your Success**

Table of Content

Introduction

What is Hypnosis

T here have been many definitions of what hypnosis is. The American Psychological Association has defined hypnosis as a cooperative interaction where the hypnotist will give suggestions to the person; he picks which he or she will respond to. Edmonton said that a person is simply but in a deep state of mind when undergoing hypnosis. Hypnosis is, therefore, when a person enters a state of mind in which a person finds himself or herself vulnerable to a hypnotist's suggestions. Hypnosis is not new to us because many people have seen it in movies, cartoons, or been to magic shows or performances where participants are told to do usual acts, and they do it. For sure, some people believe that hypnosis exists and would do anything to avoid being a victim, while others believe that its fiction.

Induction

Induction is considered as stage one of hypnosis. There are three stages in total. Induction aims to intensify the partaker's expectations of what follows after, explaining the role they will be playing, seeking their attention, and any other steps needed during this stage. There are many methods used by hypnotists to induce a participant to hypnosis. One of them is the "Braidism" technique, which requires a hypnotist to follow a few steps. This technique is named after James Braid. The first step would be to find a bright object and hold it in your left hand and specifically between the middle, fore, and thumb fingers.

The object should be placed where the participant will fix their stare and maintain the stare. This position would be above the forehead. It is always crucial that the hypnotist remind the partaker to keep their eyes on the object. If the participant wonders away from the object, the process will not work. The participant should be focused entirely on the item. The participant's eyes will begin to dilate, and the participant will start to have a wavy motion. A hypnotist will know that his participant is in a trance when the participant involuntarily closes his or her eyelids when the middle and forefingers of the right hand are carried from the eyes to the object. When this does not happen, the participant begins again, guiding that their eyes are close when the fingers are used in a similar motion. Therefore, this puts the participant in an altered state of mind. He or she is said to be hypnotized. The induction technique has been considered not to be necessary for every case. Research had shown that this stage is not as important as already known when it came to the induction technique's effects. Over the years, there have been variations in the once original hypnotic induction technique, while others have preferred to use other alternatives. James Braid's innovation of this technique still stands out.

Suggestion

After Induction, this follows the suggestion stage. James Braid left out the word suggestion when he first defined hypnosis. However, he described this stage as attempting to draw the partaker's conscious mind to focus on one central idea. James Braid would start by minimizing the functions of different parts of the partaker's body. He would then emphasize using verbal and non-verbal suggestions to get the partaker into a hypnotic state. Hippolyte Bernheim also shifted from the physical form of the partaker. This well-known hypnotist described hypnosis as the Induction of a particular physical condition, which increases one's susceptibility to the participant's suggestions. Suggestions can be verbal or one that doesn't involve speech. Modern hypnotist uses a different form of suggestions that include non-verbal cues, direct verbal suggestions, metaphors, and insinuations. Non-verbal suggestions that may be used include changing the tone, mental imagery, and physical manipulation. Mental imagery can take two forms. One consists of those that are delivered with permission and those that are done none the less and are more authoritarian.

When discussing hypnosis, it would be wise if one would be able to distinguish between the conscious mind and the unconscious mind. While using suggestions, most hypnosis will try and trigger the conscious mind other than the unconscious mind. In contrast, other hypnotists will view it as a way of communicating with the unconscious mind. Hypnotists such as Hippolyte Bernheim and James Braid, together with other great hypnotists, see it as trying to communicate with the conscious mind. This is what they believed. James Braid even defines hypnosis as the attention that is focused upon the suggestion. The idea that a hypnotist will be able to creep into your unconscious mind and order you around is next to impossible as according to those who belong to Braids school of thought. The determinant of the different conceptions about suggestions has also been the nature of the mind. Hypnotists such as Milton Erickson believe that responses given are normally through the unconscious mind. They used the case of indirect suggestions as an example. Many of the nonverbal suggestions, such as metaphors, will mask the hypnotist's true intentions from the victim's conscious mind. A form of hypnosis that is completely reliant upon the unconscious theory is a subliminal suggestion. Where the unconscious mind is left out in the hypnosis process, then this form of hypnosis would be impossible. The distinction between the two schools of thought is quite easy to decipher. The first school of thought believes that suggestions are directed at the conscious mind will use verbal suggestions.

In contrast, the second school of thought who believe that suggestions are directed at the unconscious mind will use metaphors and stories that mask their true intentions. In general, the participant will still need to draw their attention to an object or idea. This enables the hypnotist to lead the participant in the direction that the hypnotist will need to go into the hypnotic state. Once this stage of suggestion is completed and is successful, the participant will move onto the next stage.

Susceptibility

It has been shown that people are more likely to fall prey to the hypnotist tactics than others will. Therefore, it will be noted that some people can fall into hypnosis easily, and the hypnotist does not have to put so much effort. At the same time, for some, getting into the hypnotic stage may take longer and require the hypnotist to put quite the effort. While for some, even after the continued efforts of the hypnotist, they will not get into the hypnotic state. Research has shown where a person has reached the hypnotic state at some point in their lives. They will likely be susceptible to the hypnotist's suggestions, and those who have not been hypnotized, or it has always been difficult for them to reach that state. It will be likely that they may never be able to get that hypnotic state.

Different models have been established to determine the susceptibility of partakers to hypnosis. Research done by Deirdre Barrett showed that there are two types of subjects that considered being more susceptible to hypnosis and its effects. The two subjects consist of the group of dissociates and fantasizers. Fantasizers can easily block out the stimuli from reality without the specific use of hypnosis. They daydream a lot and also spent their childhood believing in the existence of imaginary friends. Dissociates are persons who have scarred childhoods. They have experienced trauma or child abuse and found ways to put away the past and become numb. If a person belongs to this group finds him or herself daydreaming, it will be associated in terms of being blank and fantasizing. These two groups will have the highest rates of being hypnotized.

Types of Hypnosis

A hypnotist can use different types of hypnosis as a participant. Each of them will use different ways and will help with certain issues. Some types of hypnosis will assist in weight loss, while others will help a participant relax.

Traditional hypnosis

This type of hypnosis is very popular and used by hypnotists. It works by the hypnotist, making suggestions to the participant's unconscious mind. The participant who is likely to be hypnotized by this does what he is told and does not ask many or frequent questions. If one was to self-hypnotize themselves, they would do this by using traditional hypnosis. As we have said, this type of hypnosis is very popular, and this could be attributed to it not requiring much skill, and it is not technical. The hypnotist will just have the right words and just tell the participant what to do. This might pose a problem to the hypnotist where the participant is a critical thinker and can analyze a given situation.

Neuro-Linguistic Programming (NLP)

This type of hypnosis gives the hypnotist wide criteria for the methods they can use in hypnosis. The hypnotist can save time during the process as the hypnotist will just use the same thought patterns to create the problem in the participant. For example, if it is stress, the same thought pattern causing this stress will be used to counter the stress.

NLP Anchoring

To understand how anchoring works, think of a particular scent. The first time you had that scent, you were going through some feeling in which the unconscious mind attached these feelings to that scent. Through this, the scent will become the anchor for those particular feelings. Every time you heard the scent, those feelings come rushing back, triggered by the unconscious mind. This type of NLP has been useful to hypnotists in the process of hypnosis. If you won a prize or some money, for example, the hypnotist will try and recreate those feelings you had when you won the prize. While recreating these feelings, the hypnotist will ensure the participant does an action during this process. Each time the subject does the said action, they will be reminded of those feelings.

This type of NLP can motivate a person to accomplish their goals, for example, if they are trying to be healthier or lose weight. The hypnotist will create a positive anchor that is in line with the mental image of the participant. The mental picture will be that of a sexy slim body. This image will be used as the motivator to start losing weight.

NLP Flash

This technique should only be done by a certified professional because it is considered very powerful and used to alter thoughts and emotions around the participant's unconscious mind. It is deemed to be helpful to persons who experience chronic stress or are addicted to a substance. Here is what the hypnotist will do; he or she is addicted to a substance instead of it, causing some feelings of happiness the act will now cause feelings of pain.

Where the person had chronic stress, the cat will bring a sense of relaxation. Those addicted to substances such as cigarettes and alcohol will now feel pain when they take these substances, which can effectively help them get over their addiction.

Chapter 1. Hypnosis Techniques

O nce you have mastered the process of hypnosis that can often be called the long process, you can begin to use another powerful form of hypnosis to your advantage, instant hypnosis. These techniques play with the basics of the mind and what can happen to everyone from time to time daily. Have you ever gazed out of the window and simply watched the rain come down? What about listening to music that makes you feel soothed and relaxed? Maybe watching a favorite movie or television show, and you just feel yourself tune out. Often when this happens, you may not even notice that your brain has checked out. You're comfortable, relaxed, and completely absorbed in what you are doing. It happens every day and has three characteristics that are telltale signs.

1. Increased focus and concentration.

2. Increased relaxation of the body.

3. Increased access to the subconscious mind.

Hypnosis simply uses this natural state of things to put your subject into that state of mind as quickly as possible.

The Handshake Technique

This technique requires that you and the subject have some trust between you. As you will reach out your hand to shake with and then pull sharply towards yourself, you will forcefully, but calming say the word sleep as you do this. If you don't have a little trust built between you, this could just as easily backfire and make the subject tense when you pull them in. How does this technique work so easily? It works by using two different methods of inducing hypnosis: moving the subject off balance, so the brain does not have time to compute a response and giving the forceful suggestion of sleep, which seems like a good idea to the brain. People are far more suggestive than they think, and that is how this simple but powerful instant technique can work.

Falling Backward Method Technique

This form of instant hypnosis again works in the process of putting someone off balance and giving them a suggestion to follow. Instead of pulling them forward towards you, however, the subject will tip slightly backward. By following simple steps, this process can put your subject under in less than a minute:

Step 1: Ask your subject to stand with their feet together and their arms hanging loosely at the side. As they get into a position to explain what you will be doing with them step by step to know what is coming next, you will let them also know this will test their relaxation reflexes.

Step2: Move to stand directly behind your subject and place both hands on their shoulders.

Stand close enough to control them as they fall, but not close enough so that they will fall directly on you. Control the fall but don't take too much weight.

Place one foot in front of the other, and you will be able to keep the right balance to hold their weight as they fall back. Tell the subject this is just a trial run.

Step 3: Ask your subject to relax and explain that you will pull them a few inches back but that you will not let them fall. Place a strong emphasis on this fact that you will not let them fall and ask them to stay relaxed and bend their body at the ankles only, not at the waist, knees, or anywhere else.

Step 4: With your hands still on the subject's shoulders, ask them to close their eyes and pull them back only a few inches. A space of two or three inches is sufficient. Remember not to jar of force them, but allow them to gently tip backward and then rock them forward again. Keep your hands firmly on their shoulders and stand the client upright again, ensuring they regained their balance.

Step 5: If your subject seems relaxed, move on to the next step. If not, assure the subject that they have done well, and repeat the earlier step again to make certain the subject knows what to expect. You may find that certain nervous subjects might require several attempts before they're fully comfortable.

Step 6: After having them fall back, you can sit them down and use a short and brief deepening technique to make sure they are deep in hypnosis. This is usually done simply using phrases such as "move deeper and deeper into hypnosis, relax" repeat this as needed to make sure that your subject is deep into hypnosis.

The Eye Test

To confirm for both you and the subject that a state of hypnosis has been reached with an instant technique, you want to use this simple process. With your subject comfortable and sitting, follow this process:

Step 1: "You feel your eyes are very heavy and completely relaxed. Each muscle around them is now relaxed. This makes your eyelids very heavy."

Step 2: "On the count of three and not before, I will ask you to open your eyes. When I ask this, you will not be able to. You are so completely relaxed that your eyelids are too heavy. You will not be able to open your eyes because your eyelids are so heavy, and you are so relaxed that you will not even try to open them."

Step 3: "Your eyelids are closed. Heavy. Sealed shut, and you can't open them."

Step 4: "One. Your eyes are closed; your eyelids are heavy. You can't open them, not even if you try. You simply can't open them. They are too heavy, so very heavy."

Step 5: "Two. You cannot open your eyes."

Step 6: "Three. Your eyes are tightly closed. Try opening them. You cannot open them, right? Your eyelids are too heavy. Stop trying, just simply relax your eyes again, no more trying to open them. As go your eyes, so you should go your body. Relax."

When you are doing this process, you do not allow your subject to try opening their eyes for more than a second or two. If you give them too much time, they will eventually be able to force their eyes open, and once they have done that, they will come out of hypnosis. If they can open their eyes right away without any effort, they have not been put under, and you will have to start again. If this does occur and open their eyes, simply tell them it's okay and that their eyes were not relaxed enough, so you will begin again. Remember to keep a festive air.

Relaxation Technique

Therapists usually ask you to make yourself feel at home and be comfy during an introduction meeting. They may even provide you with a soft couch to lay on. Why? Are they just being courteous? The truth is, it's more than that. Therapists use relaxation as a common method to induce hypnosis. If you are relaxed, you will likely fall into a trance quicker, and your mind becomes more open to accepting suggestions. Listed are some of the usual methods to promote relaxation:

- Be comfortable.

- Lay down.

- In your head, start to count down.

- Control your breathing.

- Tense your muscles and then relax.

- Speak in a calm, soft tone.

Handshake Technique

The father of hypnotherapy, Milton Erickson, became famous for using a handshake technique to get a person into a hypnotic trance. Handshake is a common greeting, but in hypnosis, it can be more than just a gesture. Hypnotists do not just shake hands in a normal way. They interrupt the subject's mind by grabbing his wrist or pulling him forward to break the balance. Because the pattern established by the subject's mind was interrupted, the client's subconscious mind will suddenly be open to suggestions.

Eyes Cues Technique

The brain has two spheres – the conscious and creative side (right) and the practical and subconscious side (left). When we are in a conversation with someone, we look for feedback to know how they feel or react to what we say. Watch your subject's eyes. Are they looking to the right? Or are they looking to the left? Remember, when they're looking to the right, that suggests that they are conscious of the current situation. If they are looking to the left, that means they are in subconscious thought.

Visualization Technique

You can use visualization to induce your subject into a hypnotic trance and make suggestions. For instance, ask your subject to visualize a room that they know very well. Instruct them to visualize each detail in that room: the windows, the smell, the lighting, the color of the wall, the texture of the floor. Then, ask them to visualize a room they do not know, such as your office. As they struggle to remember the exact details of the room they are less familiar with, they open their minds to suggestions.

Arm Levitation Technique

You can perform this by asking your subject to close their eyes. Then, ask them to notice the difference between their arms. They might say their arms are heavy or light. Subconsciously, they will enter a trance and lift their arms or make their mind believe they have lifted their arms. Either way, induction is a success.

Sudden Shock/Falling Backwards Technique

As with the handshake technique, a subject in shock can enter into a trance. You might have heard about "trust falls." The feeling of falling backward can put the body into shock. Thus, it opens the mind to accept suggestions. Of course, you must catch your subject and be very careful not to drop him/her.

Hypnotic Trigger Technique

There are several forms of hypnotic triggers. A trigger lets the subconscious remember a desired feeling or action that is suggested while under hypnosis. Here are some examples:

- Finger snap

- Clap

- Sound of ball

- Opening eyes

- Standing or sitting

Touch Technique

In this technique, the hypnotist or psychiatrist will put the subject into a relaxed state of mind. Then, gently, the hypnotist will tap the subject's hands with his/her own with slight pressure. With a pen held directly in front of the subject, they will follow it with their eyes while visualizing a perfect place in their mind. This technique needs to be repeated several times during each session. Every after the session I have with this technique, I am always relaxed and feel better.

Chapter 2. Mind Controls Hypnotism

How to Hypnotize People

T alking about any professional hypnosis instructor, they notify their clients that a successful hypnotherapist is usually confidential. Ideally, you motivate confidence in your clients with the method of 'Personality Assurance.' In other words, the clients get to the state, whereby they feel better when you are around. Of course, this is the same when you invent the method of delivering speeches to hypnotize your audience. To start with, you need to cultivate confidence in your ability when with the audience. You portray a nervous mood at the same time.

Ideally, you tend to put your client/audience in the state. They feel like you cannot find them in the room; you portray the narratives in their minds. This could be done with the ideology of focusing your attention so carefully to ensure that your words have a real effect on their perception, consciously, and unconsciously. Changing the functioning of your immune system or blood circulation tends to be done by a competent hypnotist.

A good narrator must understand the idea of you wanting to be sufficiently convincing your listeners to concentrate on what you say. This is necessary because you need them to disassociate themselves from their concerns and situations to travel to different times, places, and opportunities with you. So, at least for a while, you tend to make them understand the benefits of implementing the new ways of seeing reality.

Helping people learn new ways of responding to life, with the aim of not letting low confidence, phobias, and attention mess them up is so useful for 'Therapy hypnosis.' You concentrate your audience's attention so selectively when you speak with power that they become hypnotic rather than purely aware of the essence of their living. Therefore, this kind of education seems more profound for people.

Avoiding the Boredom Trance

However, it appears that various kinds of trances are in the crowd. You tend to hypnotize the audience by making them be in the state of leaving the room psychologically when you aren't inspiring them. Instead, the groups will try not to obey your concept and try to avoid your voice. In most cases, they begin imagining what they will do for the day, what their next social arrangements will be like, or even what they will cook for lunch. The audience/participant tends to be disassociating, but not in the ways we would like. However, it appears that the specific technique to guide your audience in the proper direction seems to be available.

Crowd Hypnosis

Professional public presenters tend to captivate the audience with thoughts and words. Also, what they will use are the anticipation, vocabulary, narrative, and initial pace. This means that implementing the ideas for their audience to act on in the future will be their ideal objective. This method tends to be very useful when it comes to hypnotizing the audience. This means that the hypnotic speakers don't give just facts. Instead, they serve the audience with an experience that will improve how they feel, think, or even behave.

Prepare Your Speech With Words That Appeal to Feelings

'Nominalization' happens to be the term in which the people who have to travel inwards to communicate with personal meanings are called. This idea helps in hypnotizing the audience. These happen to be words like mighty, lovely, devotion, wisdom, power, and so on. What's just needed is that you ensure that you align the terms with what you mean. Ideally, such correctly used terms need to contain more than mere concrete words, but words evoke feelings.

Paint Vision of Hearing Minds Through Combining Senses

We portray a paradise-like experience to someone, the moment we hypnotize them. And indeed, in pictures, words, sounds, feelings, tastes, and as well as emotions, we dream. You need to tell what you've seen, felt, heard, and tasted when you say a story about something that has happened to you when giving speeches.

Ideally, an address becomes more elegant with the implementations of this sensory appeal. For instance, "When I heard a sickening scream, I was carrying a huge bag through the mall, I turned around and saw two giant guys trying to mug an old lady who pushed them into the realm" sounds more appropriate. Compared to this, "I went to the shopping center and witnessed a serious physical conflict."

Tell All Your Stories to Hypnotize

When there are great stories to tell, tell your viewers/audience overwhelmingly, even at the moment when you're giving a talk about molecular biology.

Fascinate With Your Voice

Think about words that have significance and relevance. So, in other words, you need to speed up with your voice at times. Then sometimes slow down a bit. Perhaps, this shouldn't happen every single time to avoid getting upset. You need to reduce the speed you implement in your words when you make an argument of significance. Then, also, you can even talk to a real hypnotist calmly and on slow delivery, periodically.

Use Suddenness

We tend to go into a hypnotic spell when we're shocked or surprised, not only when we loosen up.

Humor, as it is, tends to amuse someone. So, great speakers implement the idea of using humor because it is hypnotic. There tends to be a punch on a punch line in some other perspectives, and that is because it is surprising. Mainly, the shock is often used by the hypnotists from different stages to track subjects quickly into a hypnotic state.

Be Powerful

You can create a hypnotic state for people by merely exerting power over others. Look at how people are likely to follow a person who appears to be powerful blindly. When you do this, you can get a following, and the people following you will do what you say because they want to please you and stay in your presence.

You can use this technique among your friends, family, coworkers, and any person you have a pre-existing relationship with. You want to exert your power over time so that it does not feel too aggressive. Once you notice you have followers, start small with what you are asking. They will do it without even thinking twice about it. Over time, you can ask for larger things, and you will have no trouble getting them.

Mirroring

Now, the powerful approach works for people, you know, but what about strangers? This is where mirroring comes into play. This allows you to quickly develop a rapport with someone once they see you both have someone in common. This can almost put them into a trance because they will naturally like you and want to please you since they will perceive both of you as very similar.

To successfully use this technique, pay attention to the stranger's common phrases and body language. Look at their behaviors. Exhibit these things back at them. As you continue your interaction with them, it will not take long to notice the similarities. You do not even have to lie about things you have in common. Simply mirroring their language and behaviors is enough to get them under your spell.

Use Stories

The good stories can put people into a trance-like state. Think back to when you were a kid, and your parents would read stories to you before bed. This would induce a deep state of relaxation. The same is true when you are an adult.

As you are talking to people each day, add in some anecdotes. This shows you personally and can even give you a sense of power and authority. You want people to visualize what you are saying, so use imagery to tell your story.

For example, you want a person to move something breakable because you just do not want to risk it. Do not just ask them to move it carefully. State that you do not want the vase to be dropped since it can shatter. They will visualize the vase shattering, forcing them to not only be careful when moving it, but they will volunteer to do it. They will almost see completing the task successfully as a type of personal challenge.

Lengthy Speeches

When you want to induce hypnosis on a large group, lengthy speeches are how to do it. Think about the television evangelists you have seen. They essentially use this form of hypnosis to get people to hand over thousands of dollars every time they hold a service.

When they are delivering their speech, they take a few pauses. They use varied voice tones to annunciate points and keep people completely engrossed in what they are saying. They know what their message is, and they repeat it frequently. However, they often use different phrasing, so no one in the audience ever feels like something is being forced on them.

It is not uncommon for them to tell you exactly what to do without directly telling you to do it. When you're in this type of situation, you are so enamored with the speaker that you will do just about anything they ask. They always present their lengthy speech, and then they just pass the collection basket. They do not ask you to donate because they know you will. After all, you feel dedicated to them.

You can use this technique too. You do not need an auditorium for it either. If you need something from a person or a group of people, plan out a speech. Make sure that those you are talking to feel empowered throughout the lesson. By the time you get to the end, you have already subconsciously implanted in their minds what you want. You will not need to ask for it. You will just get it.

For example, you want people to invest in your new business idea. Give them a speech about the business, about how much starting it would mean to you, and then insert a bit of a sob story about how this is your dream. Still, financially, you cannot swing it. After listening to your dramatic speech, they will feel compelled to invest.

Stacking

This is a hypnotic technique that works because you nearly overwhelm the people you are talking to. With this technique, you essentially bombard people with information. They are learning so many new things that they do not have time to sort through it. They do not feel they need to check facts because you are speaking with such authority that they automatically believe what you are saying. By the time you end your thoughts, you have essentially put them into a trance.

Cold Reading

This is something that psychics use to convince people that they can read their minds and predict their future. You will start by making a vague statement. For example, if you know a person to be shy, you will state this. You know it is accurate, and they will elaborate, giving you further information. You will use this additional information to make other predictions essentially. Once a person feels that you have this almost clairvoyant ability, they are more prone to believe anything you tell them.

Chapter 3. Dark NLP

❛ Neuro-Linguistic Programming' (NLP) is like a user manual for the brain that helps you communicate the unconscious mind's goals and desires to the conscious self. Imagine you are in a foreign country and craving chicken wings. You go to a restaurant to order the same, but when the food shows up, it ends up being liver stew... because of a failed communication.

Humans often fail to recognize and acknowledge their unconscious thoughts and desires because many get lost in translation to the conscious self. NLP enthusiasts often exclaim, "the conscious mind is the goal setter, and the unconscious mind is the goal-getter."

The idea of being your unconscious mind wants you to achieve everything that you desire. Still, if your conscious mind fails to receive the message, you will never set the goal to achieve those dreams.

NLP was developed using excellent therapists and communicators who had achieved great success as role models. It's a set of tools and techniques to help your master communication, both with yourself and others.

NLP is the study of the human mind combining thoughts and actions with the perception to fulfill their deepest desires. Our mind employs complex neural networks to process information and use language or auditory signals to give it meaning while storing these signals in patterns to generate and store new memories.

We can voluntarily use and apply certain tools and techniques to alter our thoughts and actions in achieving our goals. These techniques can be perceptual, behavioral, and communicative. They can be used to control our minds and those of others.

One of NLP's central ideas is that our conscious mind has a bias towards a specific sensory system called the preferred representational system (PRS). Phrases like "I hear you" or "sounds good" signal an auditory PRS, whereas a phrase like "I see you" may signal a visual PRS.

A certified therapist can identify a person's PRS and model their treatment around it. This therapeutic framework often involves rapport building, goal setting, and information gathering, among other activities.

NLP is increasingly used by individuals to promote self-enhancement, such as self-reflection, confidence, social skill development, but primarily by communication.

NLP therapy or training can be delivered in language and sensory-based interventions, using behavior modification techniques customized for individuals to better their social communication and improved confidence and self-awareness.

NLP therapists or trainers strive to make their clients understand that their view and perception of the world are directly associated with how they operate in it. The first step toward a better future is a keen understanding of their conscious self and contact with their unconscious mind.

It is paramount to first analyze and subsequently change our thoughts and behaviors that are counterproductive and block our success and healing. NLP has been successfully used to treat various mental health conditions like anxiety, phobias, stress, and even post-traumatic stress disorder.

An increasing number of practitioners are commercially applying NLP to promise improved productivity and achievement of work-oriented goals that ultimately lead to job progression.

Here are some prominently used NLP techniques.

Anchoring

Try this yourself! Think of a gesture or sensation on your body (pulling your earlobe, cracking your knuckles, touching your forehead), and associating it with any desired positive emotional response (happiness, confidence, calmness, etc.), recalling and reliving the memory when you experience those emotions.

Content Reframing

This NLP technique is best suited to combat negative thoughts and feelings. With these visualization techniques, you can alter your mind to think differently about situations where you feel threatened or underpowered.

Rapport Building

Rapport is the art of generating empathy in others by pacing and mirroring their verbal and nonverbal behaviors. People like other people who they think are similar to themselves.

When you can subtly mirror the other person, their brain will fire off "mirror neurons" or "pleasure sensors" in their brains, making them feel a sense of liking for you.

Dissociation

The NLP technique of dissociation guides you in severing the link between negative emotions and the associated trigger. For instance, certain words or phrases may instantly bring back bad memories and make you feel stressed or depressed. If you can successfully identify those triggers and make an effort to detach those negative feelings, you are one step closer to healing and empowering yourself.

Future Pacing

The NLP technique of leading the subject to a future state and rehearsing the potential future outcomes to achieve the desired result automatically is called future pacing. It's a type of visualization technique or mental imagery used to anchor a change or resource to future situations by imagining and virtually experiencing those situations.

Influence and Persuasion

This is the most ambivalent NLP technique and houses a gray area between dark psychology and psychotherapy.

NLP is primarily focused on eliminating negative emotions, curbing bad habits, and resolving conflicts. Another aspect of NLP deals with ethically influencing and persuading others. Now pay attention to the word ETHICAL here.

How to Use NLP as a Useful Tool to Manipulate?

Your intentions are the only North Star in a dark and lonely ocean. It is the only thing that sets NLP apart from manipulation by serving as a useful tool to remember the actual purpose of using NLP. Studies show that your brain subtly works towards achieving them when innately aware of your goals, even when you aren't actively thinking about it. It is known as "diffused thinking" when you allow your mind to wander freely, making connections randomly. It's a process that encompasses all parts of the brain and is commonly used to solve problems and difficult concepts.

The true motive can sit undisturbed, deep in your subconscious, while your brain works around it, trying to develop ways and plans to achieve it. NLP is a set of skills that allows you as the user to be in control of your own conscious and unconscious mind.

However, that doesn't mean that NLP is unsuccessful if the user's intentions are immoral. It is possible to imbue those habits known to be practiced by historically unsavory characters, such as criminals and terrorists; thus, the patient can be fashioned into the next revolutionary terrorist who ushers in a new era completely reinvents modern violence as we know it. This is an example of the more extreme cases. Subtler manipulation, the kind that may not make headlines and morning news, can be equally deadly.

For example, consider this hypothetical scenario between two rival law firms competing for the same large client. Law firm A plans to manipulate the client's choice by presenting their rival law firm in a bad light. This is done by hiring a programmer to sit in on the regular therapy sessions of law firm B's top attorney and subtly twist the patient's view of his/her relationship with their spouse, thereby planting subconscious suggestions of problems in the relationship that do not exist. This technique would fall under the category of manipulation in court, with or without NLP.

Another instance of manipulation your brain doesn't commonly recognize because humans are sympathetic creatures is the emotional manipulation done by beggars. Though there is a percentage of 'honest' beggars, who are truly homeless and struggling to survive, there is a great majority of those whose trade is begging.

It is quite popular in the South Asian region, and the manipulators often don patchy clothes and have dirty faces. They use words and behaviors to play on the emotions to convince people that they need money. Many even go the extra mile and hire children for the day, just to rub it in. The manipulation is done so well that whether they have trained themselves in NLP techniques or not, they are very good at it.

On the other hand, NLP programmers hired to hold regular workshops in businesses (such as our hypothetical law firms, for instance) use it as a tool to help boost employee motivation, and encourage them to pick up new skill-sets that have been attributed to highly successful individuals, in a bid to improve general worker productivity and employee attitude in the company. It is a technique that has shown positive results.

Similarly, as it is used in business purposes to inspire workers, it is also commonly employed by a door-to-door salesman to sell as many products as possible and earn higher commissions.

Personal programmers work with their clients to help them repair relationships with their friends and family, rectifying and solving conflicts. NLP is also clinically utilized in curing mental illnesses like PTSD, GAD, phobias, anxieties, paranoia, and even substance abuse.

There are many more instances where NLP is employed, for good and bad, but the prevailing truth of the matter is that NLP itself is not guilty. Like any technique or product, there are users and abusers.

The thing being abused is innocent of the crime of the abuser. It's NLP abusers with evil, nefarious motives that have brought a bad name on the personal development and psychotherapy technique so well-intended by Brandler and Grinder.

Chapter 4. The Positive and Negative Aspects of Neuro Linguistic Programming

T here are both positive and negative parts of neuro phonetic programming or NLP. Tragically, not many individuals have a complete comprehension of this term, even though they are dependent upon it each and ordinary. More critically, many organizations, associations, and people who realize how to control this idea, regularly do such with exploitative aims.

NLP is the investigation of how verbal correspondence impacts the human cerebrum. The words that you hear are answerable for forming your discernments, thoughts, and even your activities. This is the essential thought behind uplifting feedback. In contemplates, uplifting statements have been appeared to make significant enhancements in mentalities and practices. Neuro etymological programming characterizes why this works.

On the other hand, negative words additionally sway the individuals who hear them. Individuals who are continually encompassed by antagonistic individuals will regularly fall prey to their negative talk. Expressions of demoralization will, as a rule, cause an individual to take on a naysayer mentality. This makes it almost certain that the individual will surrender before attempting. Something else to consider is how your own words may make you stay dormant in certain life territories. You must be cautious about discussing these things on the off chance that you are attempting to create change in specific examples or practices. Your cerebrum will accept a follow up on the very words that you express.

The absolute most noteworthy experts or NLP are significant promoting and publicizing organizations. They realize that their words can shape popular suppositions and free activity. To get mass-market consideration for explicit merchandise, a significant number of these elements will make individuals partner industrialism with satisfaction. Individuals at that point start to accept that they should purchase items to feel glad.

When you have an away from how verbal correspondence influences your practices, it is critical to be progressively cautious about the words you express and the organization you keep. You can likewise play a progressively active job as an audience. Individuals who listen inactively to verbal messages are unmistakably progressively liable to being influenced by them.

When you realize what neuro phonetic programming or NLP is and how it tends to be utilized, you can become much progressively amazing in your dynamic. You will be able to begin utilizing positive words to fortify yourself and the people around you. You will furthermore turn out to be progressively capable in endeavors to prevent you or to persuade you to burn through cash on superfluous things. This is genuinely one of those occurrences in which information is power.

How Negative Thinking Can Affect Us

Negative reasoning influences us inwardly, however, genuinely. To be sure, negative considerations have genuine implications past simply the idea itself. How might you use neuro etymological programming and entrancing to break liberated from this?

Neuro semantic writing computer programs are methods by which you can truly be instructed to "retrain" how you think. A specialist prepared in NLP can assist you with rethinking and repeat contemplations, and think about them from an alternate perspective, so you truly start to think in various manners that are increasingly adjusted and positive - and without a doubt, progressively practical.

This is an extremely positive advance to take because so regularly, negative considerations are "outside of any relevant connection to the issue at hand" based on what is truly occurring.

Negative Thinking in Every Day Situations

Suppose, for instance, that you've been doled out a venture grinding away, and you're sure you can do it. You complete the activity, and you've done quite well. In any case, you notice one modest mistake. In a split second, you start to converse with yourself adversely, disclosing that you took care of the activity inadequately, even though the one small mistake isn't huge and won't sway on the nature of the undertaking generally. So while your supervisor is stating, "Incredible employment!" you may be stating to yourself, "No, it's most certainly not. I'm so dumb. I will lose my employment on account of that botch."

How Reasonable Is That?

A certified NLP Practitioner may challenge you with this: "All in all, your manager has advised you will lose your employment since you committed one little error?" How will you respond? You'll think, "Obviously not!" and understand that your supervisor is revealing to you that you've worked superbly. Like this, neuro etymological programming truly shows us how to retrain our musings in a progressively adjusted and positive manner, given a target assessment of the natural conditions.

Presently, I don't get this' meaning regarding how you can abstain from following this example by and large? All things considered you make a stride back and take a gander at the task with target eyes. Impartially, without that negative self-talk, you can see that genuinely, you worked superbly and committed one little error. What's more, even though you need to abstain from committing errors, they do occur.

So a good repetition of your underlying response - that you took care of the activity inadequately - may be to state, "I worked admirably and committed one little error. I will focus next time and make an effort not to commit a similar error, yet I can at present be pleased with what I did, all things being equal." You can likewise disclose to yourself that because your supervisor is content with what you did, you ought not exclusively to be glad for what you've done, however. You can be secure that your activity is protected. Truth be told, what is sensible and present and is considerably more precise as self-talk than your past explanation.

Chapter 5. Understanding Body Language

What is Body Language

We sometimes do things unconsciously, much like a nervous habit, such as tapping your foot or rubbing your hands together. Though we may not be aware that we are doing these things, others see these habits and read into them. We may be seen as nervous or agitated by others due to these unconscious behaviors that we are prone to.

At other times, we might engage in an action or pose with a specific intent consciously chosen. We can choose to turn our bodies towards someone we are busy talking to seem more attentive. Imagine your first job interview: you cautiously keep yourself from twitching, rubbing your face, or reclining. You have been made aware by various knowledgeable people such as school counselors and career guides to be aware of these interview bombs. Knowing how bad these make you seem, you learn not to engage in this form of body language.

We can lie with a written and spoken language. Usually, we lie to avoid getting into trouble. Likewise, we can also lie in our bodies. We can project a disingenuous body image and has been carefully polished to accomplish a particular appearance. I imagine that several of us have been caught in a scam at some point in time. This is an ideal example of how intelligent users of body language can manipulate it to convince us of their honesty. We get people to believe us based on what we show and not what we say.

In expressing emotions, the facial expression is essential. It combines the cheeks' movement, nose, lips, eyebrows, and eyes to show a person's various moods. Some researchers showed that body and facial expressions complement each other in interpreting emotions. Some experiments recognized the influence of body expression in identifying facial expression, which means that the brain simultaneously processes body and facial expressions.

Body postures can also detect emotions. If an individual is angry, he will try to dominate another person. His posture will show such approach tendencies. If he is fearful, his approach will be that of avoidance. He will feel submissive and weak.

Even gestures have different interpretations. For instance, if an individual folds his arms during a discussion, it's going to mean that he's unwilling to concentrate on the speaker or features a closed mind. If he crosses his arms over the opposite, it means he lacks confidence and is insecure.

Simple hand gestures show that the individual is self-assured and confident, while clenched hands can mean either angry or stressed. If he wrings his hands, it means he is anxious and nervous.

Finger gestures show the overall well-being of an individual. In some cultures, it is acceptable to point with an index finger. Handshakes also show the levels of emotion and confidence of individuals. They are popular in some cultures. In Muslim cultures, a man cannot shake or touch the hands of a woman. In Hindu cultures, a man greets a woman by keeping his hands together, like praying.

When it comes to learning how to read body language, the main goal is to determine if the person in front of you is genuine. Body language clues are incredibly crucial when deciphering someone's innermost thoughts, personality, and even intentions. In many ways, body language teaches you to become a human lie detector. Humans can be great liars, but while we may have been able to trick our mind into saying words we do not mean, we cannot trick our bodies into executing the lie flawlessly.

Reading body language is an excellent skill to have in job interviews when trying to solve a crime or resolve conflict. Being able to see beneath the surface into what is going on inside someone's mind will help you make better, more informed decisions.

What makes body language so tricky to master is deciphering body language cues within the right context. For example, when a person crosses his or her arms in front of the chest, you could construe that as negative body language, perhaps an indicator that the person is not happy to be here. However, depending on the context, it could also mean that the person feels cold, uncomfortable, or frustrated. Not accounting for a situation can lead to misreading of body language cues and a wrong conclusion.

Most people generally display a few categories of body language:

Dominant: Dominant body language comes into play when someone wants to be in command. The most standout cue for this category of body language is standing tall, with chest puffed out.

Attentive: This shows someone's interest and engagement with the conversation or situation.

Bored: A typical representation of this body language is the lack of eye contact and constant yawning.

Aggressive: An aggressive person will display threatening body language cues.

Defensive: A defensive person will look as if he or she is protecting or withholding information.

Closed Off: You can recognize a closed-off person by noticing if he or she is shutting you off by crossing his or her arms and guardedly standing farther away from you.

Open: This body language is friendly and welcoming.

Emotional: We usually display this body language when we feel heavily influenced by current feelings and typically have to change moods.

The Power of Body Language

Body language extends beyond more than just the four types. It can also be divided into positive and negative body language. Positive body language draws people towards you and creates a sense of belonging and accomplishment. This includes encouraging smiles, firm handshakes, making eye contact, facing someone with your body in a neutral position, and using an encouraging tone of voice.

Negative body language is based on avoidance. It includes turning your back on someone, not facing the speaker, looking down, using a soft and insecure tone of voice, and avoiding eye contact. When someone uses this body language tells, we begin to assume the worst about that person. We see them as being dishonest, uninvested, and disinterested.

Knowing these two forms of body language, which would you choose to look at? In all likelihood, you would prefer seeing positive body language. We want to feel acknowledged and valued during our communications with other people. Seeing someone face you, look you in the eye, speak in a clear tone without hiding their mouth, and have a natural appearance due to their open posture is very encouraging and ensures that communication can happen harmoniously and smoothly.

Yet, we often use negative body language when we feel intimidated or unsure of a situation. Being skilled at using your body language would help you achieve more favorable outcomes from your daily interactions and communications.

According to Guilbeault (2018), body language's power lies in that it can help you gain things you want, such as friends or jobs; however, it can also make you lose the things you want negative body language forms. It can cost you your job, friends, and even intimate relationships. Without even opening our mouths, we can attract or repel people.

Body language can build trust, which is the crucial ingredient in all relationships, whether for work, companionship, or intimacy. Using the power of body language, you can lead a more productive and successful life. Hence, it is well worth learning how to recognize body language and its meaning in others and ourselves.

Characteristics of Body Language

In general, body language manifests an individual's emotions, meaning another person can perceive it.

First, it is understood that the signal from the body language to the receiver can be highly complicated. An individual's body language consists of multiple body parts moving or not moving together. All must be taken into account to interpret a specific person's emotion. A specific facial expression taken out of context from the person's other bodily reactions will give an incomplete or otherwise misleading analysis of their emotions.

Another characteristic is that the projected emotion from body language is perceived automatically in a way similar to speech. This characteristic makes nonverbal interaction spontaneous. There is often little need to interpret further what an individual means with their body language.

A third characteristic is that young individuals can acquire and develop body language very easily and rapidly. Children learn what gestures and facial expressions mean from their parents, friends, and even strangers who interact with them. The ease of acquiring knowledge of body language can make children carry on specific body language into their maturity.

Deciphering Body Language

To understand and use body language, you have to learn how to read it in action and view it holistically as an overall picture of what a person is trying to communicate. If you want to begin controlling your body language, you'll have to understand how it all works together in the field as well. Somebody crossing their legs away from you could mean they are shy, it could mean that they are closed off to you, or it could just mean they need to pee desperately. To be able to read what they are feeling, you need to notice how they use the space around them, group behavioral actions into clusters (clusters are multiple body language cues placed together, so if they cross their legs away from you, cross their hands, and face in a direction away from you, it isn't looking good!), and to place them into context.

Actively Listening

Suppose you are looking at somebody's posture or trying to pick up the micro-expressions in their face that occur at one-fifth of a second. In that case, you might be closer to understanding how they feel, but you might also be ignoring something more obvious. The whole point of studying body language is to understand better what people think to build a better connection. The point isn't to make you paranoid that they are continually deceiving you. It's to make you less paranoid about what they are thinking.

Proxemics

Proxemics is a fancy word used in the body language community to mean the study of personal space and proximity. You can't indeed read someone's body language without noticing where they concern you in space.

Someone seems to be paying attention to you. They have open body language. They are even pointing themselves towards you– so they're paying attention to you, right? Well, maybe not if they're on the other side of the room and not moving any closer towards you.

When it comes to reading other people, some aspects of personal space are apparent. If someone is close, it will mean they are or are trying to be more intimate. However, with some people, especially men, there is a tendency to be territorial and to feel they have more access to your personal space than you might feel comfortable with. You can use these cues to determine if someone is aggressive, friendly, or flirtatious. By reading the rest of someone's body language, you can see if they are leaning towards you to be friendly or assertive. It is quite risky to invade other people's personal space to get an advantage over them. In general, try to avoid getting too close to someone unless they invite you to by touching you or speaking at a lower volume that requires you to lean in.

Chapter 6. Deception

What is Deception?

The definition is a theme that usually resonates within the spectrum of dark psychology. Throughout the years, it has been defined as any particular act used by a particular manipulative individual to instill certain beliefs within the victim that are usually false or only those possessing partial truths. It is usually placed in the same category as deceit, mystification, and suffrage. Deception is not usually an easy theme to understand since it involves many different things like, for example, distractions, propaganda camouflage, and concealment. The manipulator is often able to easily control the subject's mind since the victim is often led to placing immense trust in this manipulative individual. The victims often believe in whatever the manipulator will say and might even be basing plans and shaping their world base on the things that the manipulator is feeding their subconscious mind. This strong element of trust towards the manipulator can quickly fade away once the victim realizes what is going on. Because of this very reason, a certain level of skill is needed for deployment of this theme, since only then will a manipulator be able to skillfully change the focus of suspicion towards him and onto the victim's paranoia.

In most cases, deception will often present itself in relationship settings and lead the victim to have dominant feelings of distrust and betrayal between the partners in the relationship. This usually happens because deception is a theme that violates most of the rules of most relationships, together with having a negative influence on the expectations that come with the relationship. When getting into relationships, one of the usually ordinary things is always the ease of having an honest and truthful conversation with their partner. If the then learns that one of them is beginning to show signs of deception, they might have to learn the different ways of using misdirection and distractions to pry out reliable and truthful information that they need from them. The trust would have gone into a permanent rift that will not be easy to come back from since the victim will always be questioning everything that the partner will say and do, wondering whether the story is true of fabricated. Most relationships will end as soon as the deceptive partner is found out.

As we described earlier, this form of communication relies on lies and certain omissions to make the victim believe whatever he is being led to believing by the deceptive individual. This is the case; there are five main types of deceptive tactics that are seen to exist. We shall briefly touch on each one to better understand this theme.

Concealments

Probably taking home the medal of most used type of deception, concealment is basically when the deceptive individual knowingly omits information from his often relevant and important stories to the context. They can also engage in certain behaviors that would signal to hide relevant information to the subject at that particular time. A skilled manipulator is experienced enough to know that he will have to be clever to know that it's safe not to be directly in their approach but rather insinuate the lie leading the victim to their own conclusion, which is predetermined.

Exaggeration

What can be said about this? This is where an individual, in a sense, stretches the truth a bit too much with an intended goal of leading the story towards a direction that best caters to their needs. The manipulator will make a certain scenario appear more severe than it is to avoid lying directly to their victims. This is usually done to let the victim do whatever it is they want.

Lies

This is one tactic that we, as humans, use daily for one reason or another. We are often inclined to lie as a way to avoid some form of penalty. For example, if you work in the bank and you run late because of something minor, you will be inclined to lie to your boss to keep him from cutting you lose. What then can be said to be the meaning of this? This is where an individual gives information that is all south of the actual truth. They will present this completely fabricated truth to the victim, and they will believe it.

Equivocations

This is where an individual will knowingly make a statement of a contra dictionary nature intended to lead the victim to the path of confusion on what is exactly seems to be going on. This clever tactic will allow the manipulator to save his image if he is later discovered.

Understatements

This is where an individual minimizes aspects of the truth in the particular story being told at the time. They will often approach a victim preaching how something isn't that big of a deal when it is of the utmost importance.

What drives a manipulator to the deployment of the theme of dark psychology? According to research done over the years, there are usually 3 main things that motivate an individual to use deception on others. These three motives are under the umbrella of close relationships. They include self-focused motives, relationship-focused motives, and partner-focused motives. Let's look first at the motives focused on the partner. The victim will use deception in this kind of motive to avoid harming the subject or their partner. They may also use front to protect the relationship between the victim and an outside third party, avoid worrying about something about the subject, or keep the subject's self-esteem intact. Such motivation for deception will often be seen as both relationally beneficial and socially polite.

Deception's self-focused motive. This one is not considered noble as the first one and is therefore considered more inferior to the other techniques. Rather than worrying about the victim and how they feel, the manipulator will simply think about how they feel and their self-image. The manipulator uses deception to protect or enhance their self-image in this motive. To shield the victim from criticism, embarrassment, or anger, this form of deception is used.

Finally, we shall look at the relationship-focused motive of deception. The manipulative individual will use this deception to limit any harm that could come to the relationship simply by avoiding the trauma and conflict of relationships. This form of deception sometimes helps the relationship, depending on the situation. It may be the cause of harming the relationship because it will make things more complicated. For example, if you choose to hide how you feel about supper because you don't want to get into a fight, the relationship might be helpful. On the other hand, if you have an affair and choose to keep this information to yourself, it will only complicate things in the end.

Primary Components of Deception

As much as it may be difficult to clarify which factors show clear deployment of deception, some subtle components are immediate identifiers of these themes. The victim will come to be aware of these factors only when the manipulator dispatches a direct lie. Let us now dive deep into the particulars of said components.

Disguise

The first component we shall unravel is that of disguises. What usually goes on here is that the manipulator works tirelessly until he successfully creates the impression of being someone they are not. Manipulators often resort to this tactic if they want to hide something about them so deep that no one ever finds out. This could be a dark secret or just something as harmful as someone's name. This component's popular belief is that it is simply a change of clothes, just like in the moves. However, it goes far beyond this in that it also involves a complete change of one's persona. Having a rough idea of how discuses work, let us look at a few examples of how it can be used in the process of deception.

The first instance is where the manipulator changes himself to another person so as not to be discovered. An individual will do this with a view to maybe be able to get back into a particular crowd of people who are not very fond of him, revamp their whole personality to make someone like them, or further their own goals. In some instances, disguise may be used to refer to the hiding of one's true nature in the hopes of maybe hiding the effect that appears to be unpopular with that proposal. Disguises usually have adverse effects because it is generally hiding one's true intentions for a victim. When information is withheld in this fashion, it often clouds the victim's judgment. The victim ends up having the feeling of being in control of their decisions when they have been swayed towards the directions' manipulator. This is seen mainly in a political setting.

Camouflage

This is where individual works tirelessly to hide the truth in one way or another, leaving his victim clueless as to what exactly is going on. This is characterized by the manipulator's use of half-truths when divulging certain information to his victim. The victim will only be aware that camouflage has taken place when the actual truths are brought to light. A skilled manipulator with a lot of experience using camouflage is more likely to bra undetected in performing certain actions.

Simulation

The third component of deception is what is commonly referred to as simulation. This is simply the process where the victim is shown continuously subject matter that is false in every way. Further on, we get to see that simulation consists of 3 other techniques that can be used. They are mimicry, distraction, and fabrication.

Fabrication is when the manipulator takes something found in actual reality and chafes it to become this completely different thing. The manipulator will seek to either give detailed events that never happened or add some exaggerations that either make it sound better or worse than it sounds. The core of their story, however, is usually true. If the teacher gives them a bad grade, these manipulators may further the story by stating that they were given the bad results on purpose. The reality is that the manipulator did not study for the test hence his bad grade.

Mimicry is another tool that manipulators use when deploying these tactics of deception. The manipulator here usually portrays a persona that is quite close to their own, but not their own. They may present an idea similar to someone else's and give him credit for thinking about it first. This form of stimulation may be able to take pace through visual and auditory stimuli.

The last tool we shall look at is that of distraction as another form of simulation in deception. This is where the manipulator tries to get the victim only to focus their attention on everything else but the truth. How is this usually done? This is generally achieved through baiting or the offering of something more tempting than the reality itself.

Chapter 7. Dark Cognitive Behavioral Therapy

"A small behavioral change can also lead to embracing a wider checklist of healthier choices" - Chuck Norris.

What is Dark CBT?

To understand Dark CBT, we first must realize the necessary cognitive behavioral therapy and its approach to mental health and healing. Dark CBT is founded on the tried and true CBT principles employed by therapists everywhere. That is why it is guaranteed to work. Learning about CBT and then applying them as you see fit to unknowing subjects makes you very powerful.

Gain a thorough understanding of how to use CBT and maybe even use it upon yourself for practice. From there, you can begin leveraging Dark CBT as a clandestine healing method or weapon on those around you.

History of CBT

CBT was first developed by a psychologist named Aaron Beck in the 1960s. Beck noticed that his patients had internal monologues, where they spoke to themselves in the privacy of their minds.

Beck began to have his patients analyze their automatic thoughts and report them. As his patients became more conscious of their ideas, they realized how these thoughts could make or break their success. Some thoughts made them make poor decisions or drew them to untrue assumptions that made them feel bad for no reason. Other studies helped them overcome problems and feel better about themselves. By gaining awareness of their thoughts by reporting them verbally to Beck or writing them down throughout the day, his patients were able to gain more control over their thinking.

In time, Beck was able to teach his patients to harness their thoughts and become more self-aware. He taught them to think differently to feel better. He noticed that changes in thinking led to changes in behavior and emotions. Correcting flawed thinking was what helped his patients heal faster.

Since Beck's initial observation, CBT has grown by leaps and bounds. It is now better understood and has become a significant part of psychotherapy. All therapists are aware of CBT, and most therapists employ it to some degree in their practice. There are many forms of CBT, but they all have the same premise and the same goal, putting them under the enormous Cognitive Behavioral Therapy umbrella.

Now we have developed Dark CBT. Dark CBT operates on the same principles as CBT. However, it is more clandestine. Rather than using CBT on yourself or a willing psychotherapy patient, Dark CBT is something you can use on anyone without their awareness. You can apply CBT concepts to change someone's thinking to suit your needs. You can also use it on yourself, emphasizing becoming successful and achieving what you want in life. Dark CBT goes beyond simple healing and instead gives you the power to shape your life and your relationships as you desire.

Your interest in using Dark CBT may be purely altruistic, as you seek to help others who won't help themselves. Or you may have a more nefarious interest in using it to get your way and to manipulate others. How you use Dark CBT is up to you entirely, but the wealth of opportunity that Dark CBT provides you with is astounding.

Dark CBT is a relatively new method. It has not been applied to many study groups or researched extensively. Therefore, there is room for growth and experimentation in Dark CBT. You may find new applications or new ways of performing Dark CBT that is already unheard of. This is a new field that you can certainly expand and make your own. Supplement your Dark CBT with simple CBT methods and experiment with trial and error. You may just find your type of therapy that works well for you, based on the incredible techniques included and in basic CBT.

Why Use CBT?

There has been much success using CBT to treat difficulties in people's lives, ranging from depression to alcoholism to drug dependency to relationship problems. It can help people quit bad habits and feel better about themselves. It can also help people learn how to cope with their mental ailments to feel better. Even people who are not mentally ill can benefit from using CBT thought processes to tackle challenging problems in their lives, such as marriage difficulties, difficulties with communication, anger management issues, and even financial struggles.

The great thing about CBT is that it is possible to use on yourself. With the help of a CBT journal, you can document your thoughts and emotional reactions to events in your life or emotional wounds you are trying to overcome, or bad habits you are trying to break free of. Then, you ask yourself questions that lead you to change how you look at the situation, wound, or habit. You write down your new mental approach and new emotions now that you are using different thinking. You will notice a drastic improvement in your feelings and outlook on life. Suddenly, you won't have so many difficulties in life, and your problems will become so easy to solve that they will practically disappear before your eyes.

Dark CBT is incredibly useful for two reasons. The first is that Dark CBT is focused on personal gains and success. Rather than just healing your annoying thinking habits, you learn to become a massive success at anything that you wish. You can make yourself invincible if you teach yourself to believe that you are capable of anything. You can also create a monster by teaching someone else to feel the same way.

The second is that Dark CBT is sneaky. So even if someone is not interested in changing his thinking, you can still use Dark CBT on him to achieve the results that you desire. You will enjoy success, and he won't even know what has happened to him. You can fix people who refuse to get help or change people who stand in your way. No one will guess what you are doing. You simply seem to be an interested friend or loved one, trying to help someone think more realistically or positively.

What Separates Dark CBT From Regular CBT?

We already talked about this a little bit. But we want to stress that Dark CBT is the same as regular CBT. Its uses and applications are a bit different, however. That is the only thing that separates the two types of CBT.

Regular CBT is used in therapy or by individuals who are actively interested in changing their thinking. People use CBT knowingly and willingly. Their desire to change can make CBT very useful. You will find that you can use CBT to correct your problems, or you can visit a therapist who will set goals for you and help you adjust your thinking. The entire process is transparent and known to all parties.

Dark CBT is more opaque, hidden by a veil of deception. The subject of Dark CBT most likely is not aware of what is going on. Dark CBT is significant because it is subliminal, and it makes someone think that there is something wrong with him so that he strives to change it. You never reveal that you are the therapist here. You are also never asked to perform Dark CBT on anyone. This can be unethical, but again, you are using Dark CBT at your own risk.

Dark CBT is not evil in and of itself. It can be used for evil, but that is your call. The altruistic and positive applications of Dark CBT can be especially useful if you choose to make someone better through Dark CBT. You can help people who can't help themselves and who are resistant to getting help. You also create your success, furthering your own goals, and getting ahead in life. You don't have to become a monster and use Dark CBT to hurt people to gain from it. Using Dark CBT as a way to help others can improve your own life because it will heal your relationships and make people like you more. People will associate you with feeling better and liking themselves more, so they will want to spend more time around you. And everyone knows that being liked by people gets you what you want.

Even if you do choose to use the darker applications for Dark CBT, you won't ever get caught. People will not be aware of what you are doing. Therefore, you won't hurt your subjects or destroy relationships. You also won't get into trouble because you are not doing anything illegal.

Chapter 8. The Art Of Using Your Mind to Succeed

M any people want to learn about dark psychology because they want to do better in their careers. They aren't content working the job they already have: they want to prove themselves capable of more.

But somewhere along the way, we figure out the truth: that getting ahead in our careers isn't necessarily a matter of skill but manipulation and persuasion. As you know, dark psychology is the best and most legitimate way to learn these skills, and now it's time to learn how to use them specifically in a work setting.

We have to think in a more challenging way about how we interact with our co-workers. For instance, let's say we have a female early 20-something analyst amid a post-graduation down-cycle who has encountered many challenges both professionally and personally since starting work a few years ago.

She frequently finds herself wanting to connect with people who are perceived to be more advanced in their careers or whose interests are different from her own. Identifying why you are attracted to certain people is a valuable skill for early-career practitioners. It likely contributes to her success as an analyst. If she wants to get ahead, she should follow along with all the directions in these pages, where we speak to dark psychology in the workplace directly.

Personality is an incredibly crucial subject for the workplace context because it is an environment where you have to interact with many different kinds of people, many of whom—you will soon find out—you don't know that well as people.

Dark psychology is broader than neurolinguistics programming, but NLP is where all of our tools and techniques of in-depth communication and manipulation come from. NLP is where the three significant steps of manipulation and mind control originate from:

- Establish your state control and perceptual sharpness.

- Imitate the unconscious cues of communication of your subject so that they incorporate you into their mind.

- Use one of the techniques.

People continuously think without even realizing it because most thought is unconscious. NLP is how we take advantage of most studies' cold nature to tell people's minds to change the structure before they even know it.

NLP's topic is vital for discussing workplace personalities because NLP has five main categories for the kinds of characters' people have. In the jargon of NLP, these "personalities" are actually called metaprograms. You would do well to identify the important people at your workplace within these metaprograms. Take advantage of your perceptual sharpness to ascertain this information.

As we have told you before, getting information about the subject is everything. But it is also true that our brains need to sort all the information we get into categories to understand the world better. These metaprograms do that job for you.

Metaprograms are more useful than personalities because they are more objective. They also focus on the motivations people have and how they use logic rather than their mannerisms or less essential behavior patterns. Metaprograms do not merely describe how much you like attention or how nervous or relaxed you are. You may notice some aspects of each metaprogram that overlap with these traits. Still, metaprograms are more specific than these less useful terms.

These NLP-styled personalities are not only a way for you to get more information about your co-workers. Remember the second step of NLP's mind-reading and manipulation: you have to imitate the communications cues the subject shows you. When you do this, you make them unconsciously see you as being like themselves. That means if you take on the traits of your co-worker's metaprogram, you make it easier for you to succeed in this step.

The last thing for you to know about metaprograms, in general, is that they are sorted in dichotomies. A dichotomy is a contrast between two items that are different. But while you should choose just one from each dichotomy in each metaprogram, you must remember that people are not as simple as being A or B. Any time we have a dichotomy—in any situation—picking one of the two is just a category you can use to simplify things and think of them differently. But you should not think of them as being always or exclusively one of the two. People are much more complicated than this.

Our first metaprogram is between the dichotomy of options and procedures. People who are on the options metaprogram don't like being limited or being told what to do. They want as much freedom as possible, and they like to think about things from a general perspective rather than getting in the weeds. On the other hand, people on procedures need to understand every small detail whenever they get into something new. Procedures people hate the feeling that they are missing something. When an element is skipped, they fear they are missing something important.

The second metaprogram is external and internal. This metaprogram is concerned with people's incentives. External people want to be told by others when they do good work, and they want to be notified when they do bad work, too. Internal people don't want to get outside opinions about their work, though. They feel they know when their work is good or not, and hearing what other people think is just a bother.

The third dichotomy in metaprograms is proactive and reactive. These metaprograms describe how someone deals with the future. Reactive people look at a calendar and are always thinking about how the work they are doing. Now fits into the picture of all of their work. This can be a hindrance because they believe so much about planning to lose sight of what they are trying to do right now. Proactive people, on the other hand, hate thinking about the future or planning ahead. They only care about the here and now.

Our second-to-last is toward and away. This metaprogram is about goals and deterrents. All of us have things we look forward to in the future, but toward people are chiefly concerned about their goals, and they don't look behind them at all. Away people are the exact opposite of this. They can have issues looking ahead because they spend so much time thinking about what is behind them.

Finally, we have sameness and difference. Sameness people have a love for familiarity: they spend their time around things they already know. Things they don't know will make them fearful, so these people avoid them at all costs. On the other hand, different people are always craving new experiences to have new people meet, fresh foods to eat, etc. If there is something they haven't experience yet, different people want to share it.

These are the five significant dichotomies in metaprograms. Whoever the co-worker is who you want to use our dark psychology tricks on will want to sort them into these metaprograms. Now, when you use the Aristotelian technique of envisioning the future, you have a more objective stand-in for the person you will interact with.

When we imagine someone in our heads, it isn't always accurate to how they are. NLP's metaprograms are useful because they make us think carefully about our subject's kind of person.

Metaprograms are particularly useful for the work environment because they force us to think about the people we work with more objectively. When you do Step 1 and prepare to get into the co-worker's mind with Step 2, you can use these metaprograms to paint a fuller picture of who you will use dark psychology on.

Since these are often just people we interact with exclusively in work environments, we can be surprised by how little we might know about them from a metaprogram standpoint. If you are honest with yourself as you sort them into these dichotomies, you might realize you don't know very much about them at all. When this turns out to be the case, don't just go along with the dark psychology technique anyway. There is no point in doing this when it won't always work—you can't adapt to the social cues of a person you don't even know yet.

That's why from here, you will have to do more intel-gathering on them first before you can even move on to Step 1. Step 1 can't successfully happen until you know the person and how they fit into all the metaprograms. Until you do that, you won't be able to properly imagine your interactions with them for Steps 2 and 3.

With that said, after you get to know the co-workers' metaprograms, let your senses do all the work in perceptual sharpness, use our exercises to prepare your state control, and imagine the interaction in your imagination, you are ready for Step 2.

For Steps 2 and 3, things go about the same when you are dealing with someone from your workplace. However, some techniques seem tailor-made for use in the work setting. We will go over these before moving onto our big lesson on neurolinguistics programming in psychology.

We will cover three big dark psychology techniques for the workplace before diving into the world of NLP. Social framing is a technique in which we paint a picture for the subject where adopting a particular behavior or idea will help them with social climbing.

Our social lives are one of the most important things to us as humans. That's why framing the truth about the subject's social environment is such a powerful tool for manipulating and mind-controlling people. As long as we make them believe they get a social reward for doing what we say, they will jump at the opportunity.

Executing this technique is simple. Assuming you have already mentally sorted these techniques into the proper metaprograms, controlled your state, and paid close attention to your senses.

Chapter 9. Dark Personalities

D ark psychology is not a single, universally applicable medical diagnosis that can be applied across all cases of deviant personalities. In fact, there are a wide variety of ways that dark psychology may manifest itself in someone's psychological and behavioral makeup. There is no absolute division of one deviant personality type from another. Many bizarre personalities with prominent dark psychology features may display more than one manifestation of dark psychology.

We will explore three types of dark psychology personalities. It is important to remember that although the internet has spawned a massive growth in problems resulting from dark psychology, these traits have been part of human culture since ancient times. One of the dark psychology profiles we will explore here, Machiavellianism, takes its name from a medieval politician. Another narcissism takes its name from an ancient mythological character. Together, the three dark psychology profiles talked about here—psychopathy, Machiavellianism, and narcissism—make up what is known as "the Dark Triad."

The Dark Triad Personalities

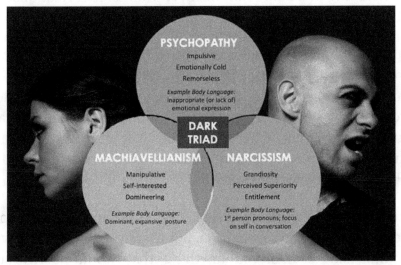

Narcissism

The term "narcissism" originates from an ancient Greek myth about Narcissus, a young man who saw his reflection in a pool of water and fell in love with the image of himself. In clinical psychology, narcissism as an illness was introduced by Sigmund Freud and has continually been included in official diagnostic manuals as a description of a specific type of psychiatric personality disorder.

In psychology, narcissism is defined as a condition characterized by an exaggerated sense of importance, an excessive need for attention, a lack of empathy, and, as a result, dysfunctional relationships. Commonly, narcissists may outwardly display a too high level of confidence. Still, this façade usually hides a very fragile ego and a high degree of sensitivity to criticism. There is often an enormous gulf between a narcissist's highly favorable view of himself or herself, the resulting expectation that others should extend to him or her favors and special treatment, and the disappointment when the results are quite negative or otherwise different. These problems can affect all areas of the narcissist's life, including personal relationships, professional relationships, and financial matters.

As part of the Dark Triad, those who exhibit traits resulting from Narcissistic Personality Disorder (NPD) may engage in relationships characterized by a lack of empathy. For example, a narcissist may demand constant comments, attention, and admiration from his or her partner but will often appear unable or unwilling to reciprocate by displaying concern or responding to their partner's circumstances, thoughts, and feelings.

Narcissists also display a sense of entitlement and expect excessive reward and recognition, but usually without ever having accomplished or achieved anything that would justify such feelings. There is also a tendency toward excessive criticism of those around him or her. Combined with heightened sensitivity when even the slightest amount of criticism is directed at him or her.

Thus, while narcissism in popular culture is often used as a pejorative term and an insult aimed at people like actors, models, and other celebrities who display high degrees of self-love and satisfaction. NPD is a psychological term that is quite distinct from merely having high self- esteem. The key to understanding this aspect of dark psychology is that the narcissist's image of himself or herself is often completely idealized, grandiose, and inflated and cannot be justified with any real, meaningful accomplishments or capacities make such claims believable. As a result of this discord between expectation and reality, the demanding, manipulative, inconsiderate, self-centered, and arrogant behavior of the narcissist can cause problems not only for themselves but also for all people his or her life.

Machiavellianism

Strictly defined, Machiavellianism is the political philosophy of Niccolò Machiavelli, who lived from 1469 until 1527 in Italy. In contemporary society, Machiavellianism is a term used to describe the popular understanding of people who are perceived as displaying very high political or professional ambitions. In psychology, however, the Machiavellianism scale is used to measure the degree to which people with deviant personalities say manipulative behavior.

Machiavelli wrote The Prince, a political treatise. He stated that sincerity, honesty, and other virtues were indeed admirable qualities. In politics, the capacity to engage in deceit, betrayal, and other forms of criminal behavior was acceptable if there were no other means of achieving political aims to protect one's interests.

Popular misconceptions reduce this entire philosophy to the view that "the end justifies the means." To be fair, Machiavelli himself insisted that the more critical part of this equation was ensuring the end itself must first be justified. Furthermore, it is better to achieve such ends using means devoid of treachery whenever possible because there is less risk to the actor's interests.

Thus, seeking the most effective means of achieving a political end may not necessarily lead to the most treacherous. Also, not all political fortunes that have been justified as worth pursuing must be pursued. In many cases, the mere threat that a particular course of action may be followed may be enough to achieve that end. In some cases, the betrayal may be as mild as making a credible threat to take action that is not intended.

In contemporary society, many people overlook the fact that Machiavellianism is part of the "Dark Triad" of dark psychology and tacitly approve of the deviant behavior of political and business leaders who can amass great power or wealth. However, as a psychological disorder, Ma- Machiavellianism is entirely different from a chosen path to political power.

The person displaying Machiavellian personality traits does not consider whether his or her actions are. The most effective means of achieving their goals, whether there are alternatives that do not involve deceit or treachery, or even whether the ultimate result of his or her actions is worth achieving. The Machiavellian personality is not evidence of a strategic or calculating mind attempting to reach a worthwhile objective in a contentious environment. Instead, it is always on, whether the situation calls for a cold, calculating, and manipulative approach or not.

For example, we had all called in sick to work when we just wanted a day off. But for most of us, such conduct is not how we usually behave. After such acts of dishonesty, many of us feel guilty. Those who display a high degree of Machiavellianism would not just lie when they want a day off; they see lying and dishonesty as the only way to conduct themselves in all situations, regardless of whether doing so results in any benefit.

What's more, because of the degree of social acceptance and tacit approval granted to Machiavellian personalities who successfully attain political power, their presence in society does not receive the kind of negative attention accorded to the other two members of the Dark Triad—psychopathy and narcissism.

Psychopathy

Psychopathy is defined as a mental disorder with several identifying characteristics: antisocial behavior, amorality, an inability to develop empathy, establish meaningful personal relationships, extreme egocentricity, and recidivism, with repeated violations resulting from an apparent failure to learn from the consequences of earlier transgressions. In turn, antisocial behavior is defined as behavior based upon a goal of violating formal and/or informal rules of social conduct through criminal activity or through acts of personal, private protest, or opposition, all of which are directed against other individuals' society in general.

Egocentricity is the behavior when the offending person sees himself or herself as the central focus of the world, or at least of all dominant social and political activity. Empathy is the ability to view and understand events, thoughts, emotions, and beliefs from others' perspectives. It is considered one of the most essential psychological components for establishing successful, ongoing relationships.

Amorality is entirely different from immorality. An immoral act is an act that violates established moral codes. An immoral person can be confronted with his or her actions with the expectation that they will recognize that their actions are offensive from a moral, if not a legal, standpoint. Amorality, on the other hand, represents psychology that does not realize that any moral codes exist, or if they do, that they have no value in determining whether or not to act in one way or another.

Thus, someone displaying psychopathy may commit horrendous acts that cause tremendous psychological and physical trauma and not ever understand that what he or she has done is wrong. Worse still, those who display signs of psychopathy usually worsen over time because they cannot connect the problems in their lives and the lives of those in the world around them and their own harmful and destructive actions.

The Dark Triad in Practice

The professional workplace has acknowledged the presence of people exhibiting Dark Triad characteristics.

The following diagram illustrates that they are tolerated for their efficiency and their ability to get things done but contrasts that ability with the adverse effects it has on their ability to form personal relationships:

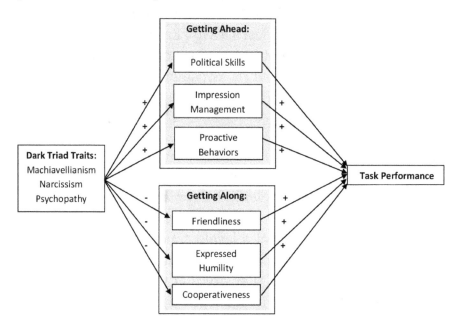

(Benjamin McLarty, Mississippi State University, 2015)

The remainder will discuss a wide variety of people and situations where you may find one, two, all three, or some combination of these Dark Triad personalities working in concert around you.

The clinical descriptions are easy enough to categorize. In isolation, it can be reasonably straightforward to separate one type of dark psychology from another. The real world is a lot messier. Many of us have grown accustomed to so-called "toxic relationships," whether they are relationships with our partners, co-workers, family members, bosses, or political and community leaders.

Also, dark psychology manifestations are often far more mundane than the dramatic examples we see in major television and film productions about serial killers and other criminals' romantic lives. The more we accept these relationships, as usual, the more difficult it will be to identify them as problematic.

Remember that psychological, emotional, and social predators do not think of themselves as sick. Their lack of morality and empathy, and their adaption from a very early age to live according to rules and methods you may find wrong, can make their presence intimidating. However, you should also remember that even when their amorality and lack of empathy may allow them to enjoy it. An unfair advantage in relationships, their mental capacities result from underdevelopment, not a higher evolutionary state.

Chapter 10. The Dark Triad

The dark triad is a psychology term that refers to a person's behavioral characteristics, which is, in most cases, defined as narcissism, Machiavellianism, and psychopathy. Some people rate it as a mental disorder and some as a disaster that just dawns on someone changing their behavior and how they relate to others. Dark triad generally affects a person's personality, making them take advantage of others. People with these traits tend to be manipulative, deceptive, and egoistic. They attempt to brainwash others to gain success and fame.

Politicians are, on most occasions, the worst group of people affected by this personality disorder. Their lives are full of lies, ego, and manipulation. To gain power, most of them only deceive other people to get public support and seem successful. Many people fall victim to the dark triad because they are not well exposed to the point of understanding what it is. They cannot easily tell when this is being used against them.

Persons with dark triad personalities have no empathy for others. They always attempt to have everything for themselves, ignoring other people's importance around them. Narcissists still want to be regarded as the most influential people in society. They want to be praised and admired all the time, a kind of behavior that only manipulates others for the benefit of their interests.

You may be tempted to think that these people are insane. From my perspective to some extent, they are. No one in his normal state of mind would want to have everything go their side at the expense of others. To these people who possess a Machiavellianism trait, they always want to win and be declared successful. They go as far as deceiving everyone around them to turn out the right person. They easily exploit the "less fortunate" in society to open their ways.

Apart from politicians, bloggers are another group of people that are overwhelmed by these traits. For example, in Kenya, we have Dr. Miguna, who is all over the social media busy manipulating people—the youth and young politicians being the most affected. He tries to make everyone his psychopath through his blogs, twits, books, and constant drama here and there.

Can we Say Dr. Miguna is insane? He is all over seeking fame and wants everyone to believe he is always right, and the rest are wrong. He manipulates everyone, and those who follow his steps end up being disappointed at the end. Once he gets what he is looking for, he turns against you and uses your negatives to manipulate others that are not in the same line as him. He comes up with dramas to attract attention and convince everyone to believe whatever he does.

While politicians everywhere are fighting him back, the youth become psychos by his blogs and believe that he is right because he is fighting politicians whom he claims to be narcissists. Not to be personal, I would like to say that if you research deeply into psychology, you will find most bloggers with the same interest showing narcissism, Machiavellianism, and psychopathy traits. They won't feel guilty or ashamed because they don't even notice that they are too much.

Anyone can be a victim of these traits. You may, at one point in your life, find yourself in a relationship with a narcissist. Before you notice it, you will be exploited and used by your partner. Your partner can be that antagonistic person that only feels superior to you and those around you. They will always want to be treated special and can exploit you to serve their interests. They often interact in a way that shows you are less important and not as good as them.

This kind of person usually wants to be listened to. They will prefer seeking attention than empathizing with you or even recognizing your needs. Everything they do is always for their benefit. They only concentrate on feeling better in the relationship and are never ready to give you a listening year. You have no say in their decisions because this makes them feel less important to you and don't respect their decisions.

To know that you are in a relationship with a narcissist, you will realize that your partner doesn't really care about how you feel. They only expect you to make them happy and superior without considering what you go through for them to be what they want. Failing to meet their interests makes them feel so low and unwanted in the relationship. They make you feel like you are of no good to them and that you don't deserve them.

They can also be antisocial and low self-esteemed. They will always think of their mistakes as the worst ever and that none can be compared. Whenever they fail in something, they will feel like they don't fit in society anymore and imperfect. They feel so drowned and depressed as a result of one mistake. This is always brought about by the fear of being a normal person.

On some occasions, narcissists attempt to praise themselves too much without realizing how majestic they can be. They never stop talking about their achievements and plans in life. They always talk about how intelligent and successful they are and even exaggerate what they are capable of. They always want people to believe that their success cannot be related to someone else's. Stopping them from doing this makes them feel stupid, and they can easily hate you for pinpointing their imperfections.

These persons' living standards are always set high by them, which is becoming realistic because they are in a way that has low standards. Their lives are usually filled with a fantasy about success, and they expect everyone around them to respect them because their destinies are thought to be successful. No one can ever change their perception in their minds without hurting them and making them feel useless.

At some point, these people are always depressed, and no one will ever understand the reason for their depression. Understanding them becomes difficult. If you are not a psychologist, you will always be brainwashed to serve their interests before noticing what you are getting yourself into. Other people can advise you, but you will not have the time to listen to what they have to say because you will have fallen victim to narcissism. The narcissist will, by that time, have full control of you.

You are always left torn between thoughts when it reaches a point that you no longer understand a friend or a partner who has a dark personality. Failing to listen to them makes them feel worse than other people while listening to you is useless to them, on the other hand. They never have time to listen to you but to seek the audience all the time.

Machiavellian leaders are the most dangerous leaders because they are always cunning and duplicitous. They always manipulate everyone from doing what they want, whether they like it or not, and never reveal any reason for their actions. They only do that when the favor is on their side. They always make people believe that they are the most intelligent and that no one's intelligence can be compared to theirs. Those who believe in this kind of leaders are never ready to listen to other people's advice unless they align with the Machiavellian heads.

Dark triad strikes too much due to several reasons and the following additional reasons.

1. The Understanding of Dark Triad Is Not Everybody's Cup of Tea

Not everyone has the psychology of understanding dark personality. This leads to many of us fall victim to dark triads without noticing it. We get manipulated easily and exploited to serve the interest of narcissists and Machiavellian leaders without a choice of thinking a second time or even the chance to take an alternative move.

2. The Fear of Standing Alone

Narcissists always manipulate the big number from being on their side and supporting their ideas. This has left many people stranded between thoughts because they fear being left alone for making an opposing decision. They fear of not getting back up from those around you led many people to fall, victims of the dark triad since they are forced to take steps they were not ready to take.

This usually happens with people who are often close to this kind of person or whose friends are involved with those with dark personalities.

3. I Don't Want to Lose a Friend

Many people tend to value friendship more than their own safety. They are too much into their friend's decisions and way of life that they even forget they are also important. Such people are the most common victims of the dark triad. They easily get exploited by their friends into doing what their friends want, what makes them happy.

In this case, when you're are friends with a narcissist, then you have no choice. You will always be a tool for happiness. You will be ready to listen to all sorts of boasting and exaggerated stories from your friends.

4. Investing Your Trust in the Wrong Person

On many occasions, we don't always know the right person to trust. Laying your trust in someone without considering their personality opens a gate for you to be used by narcissists. This normally occurs in relationships that are just beginning, and partners wish to travel miles away together.

Many fall into traps of their partners because they invest too much trust in them that they can never think of the negative side of them. This is what makes the narcissists overjoyed and leave them feeling so highly of themselves.

5. Believing Too Fast

These narcissists always have their stories told everywhere by them and by those who believe helplessly in them. They always catch the interests of those who believe in all stories they are told because they believe the people telling the story are always right, intelligent, and successful.

The narcissist always catches others' attention with their striking success that makes others believe in them desperately and follow their steps blindly without a third eye to see into the future and the consequences of following these people.

6. Most People Don't Care

The tendency of assuming everything said by those in authority is final is what makes us victims of manipulation and exploitation. Some of us don't even care about what is going on around them, and having no idea about it for them is even much better. Some say that something you don't know does not hurt.

People with dark personalities easily exploit such people because they know the favor will always be on their side no matter what. No one will stand against them because they don't even care in the first place.

7. Psychopathy

Being too possessed with someone is what leads you to become their psychopaths. You will always want to listen to what they say, and at the end of it, you will be convinced they are right, and anything said against them is wrong. You will feel pain when they are in pain are depressed when they are depressed because you have become their shadow. Whoever sees you see the person you have invested your personality in.

Conclusion

N ow that you've learned some of the basic dark psychology disciplines, you have a great deal more power than you had before. At the very least, you will be better able to recognize controlling techniques and behaviors when other people try to use them against you. If someone is trying to manipulate or even persuade you, you can now see through their tricks and resist.

But you also have the unique opportunity to use dark psychology for your personal growth and improvement. Just because these tools and techniques are labeled 'dark' doesn't mean they're inherently destructive. Many techniques, including hypnosis and NLP, were first developed as self-improvement tools. Only when people learned how to turn these techniques against other people did they become relegated to the field of 'dark' psychology.

NLP, persuasion techniques, body language, and even hypnosis are all regularly taught in social spheres that we would not normally consider 'dark.' Athletes, business people, teachers and educators, actors, entertainers, and marketers all regularly use these techniques to improve their performance, increase their productivity, make themselves better negotiators, and yes, to convince others to do what they want. There's nothing inherently amoral about social influence, especially if the thing you're persuading the other person to do is good for them. Using NLP techniques to persuade your alcoholic partner to get help is hardly an act of evil or manipulation. Neither is learning to read your teenager's body language to improve your communication and defuse potential conflict.

With great power, however, does come great responsibility. Whenever you decide to employ any of these techniques against another person, always take a step back and ask yourself, "What are the consequences for the other person if I get my desired outcome? Will the other person be hurt? Will this put them in danger? Will this compromise their core values or beliefs in some way?" If the answer to any of these three questions is yes, you have to find another way to get what you want without manipulating tactics. All of the techniques that you've learned are extremely powerful. With patience and practice, they do work. Suppose you become skilled in any of these disciplines and decide to use them for the wrong reasons. In that case, you could cause some serious damage to another person's psychological well-being and risk losing your important relationships if someone else becomes aware of what you're doing.

I hope that, you re-enter your life as a more secure and empowered person. Psychological techniques are subtle and often context-based. It's normal to be clumsy when you first begin, and you should always be aware of how the other person is responding so that you can make necessary and appropriate adjustments to your techniques.

With these tactics at your disposal, you are no longer at the mercy of other people. If you find yourself constantly rubbing other people the wrong way, perhaps receiving labels like 'bossy' or 'pushy,' you now have a variety of subtler ways to get what you want. If you're someone that's constantly fighting and barreling over others, you know that sometimes being straightforward isn't the best option. Being too blunt can often backfire on you. Asking for what you need more subtly won't only get you more success in life—it may even make it easier for you to build healthy relationships with other people.

If you find yourself in the opposite position, these tactics can work for you, too. If you feel that you're just too timid to get what you want or find yourself easily pushed around by other people, you now have a way to succeed. Instead of running headlong into conflicts that scare you, you can try a different approach, one that may feel much more comfortable. As you start to achieve results, you'll probably feel a big improvement in your confidence. And the more confident you feel, the more comfortable you will be with straightforward communication, making you a much better communicator all the way around.

Most importantly of all, now that you are aware of dark psychology, those who would wish to do you harm have significantly less power over you. Suppose someone does try to manipulate, persuade, or use NLP against you in the future. In that case, you will be better able to recognize their tactics before something bad happens. And suppose you are currently in a relationship with a manipulative person. In that case, you now have a better idea of their tactics and therefore take steps to free yourself from their influence.

CPSIA information can be obtained
at www.ICGtesting.com
Printed in the USA
BVHW040805060221
599513BV00009B/734

CONTENTS

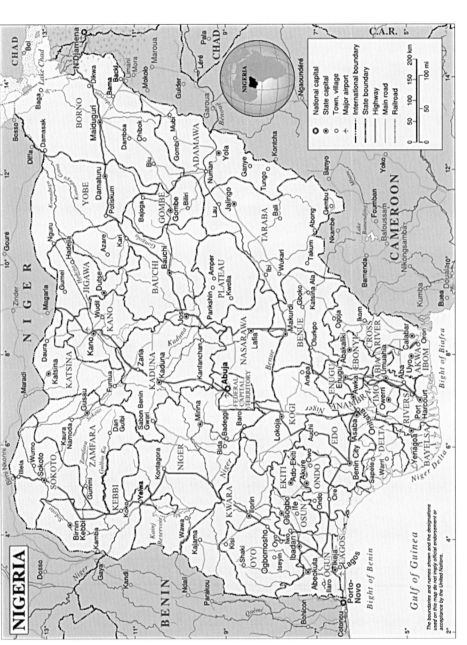

Political map of Nigeria. (UN)

TIMELINE

1960:   Nigeria becomes an independent state within the Commonwealth after sixty years of British colonial rule. The new head of state is Prime Minister Sir Abubakar Tafawa Balewa, a northerner who heads a coalition government.

1962/1963:   Two controversial censuses take place throughout the country, the first in December 1962, followed by another a few months later, both of which have roots in the differences between southern (mainly Christian and animist) and largely Muslim northern Nigeria, and fuelling regional and ethnic tensions.

1962–1965:   The Tiv tribe of Nigeria's so-called Middle Belt area of the North grow increasingly intolerant of Muslim-orientated rule and openly riot for almost three years because of perceived domination by Muslim northerners.

1964/1965:   The general election that takes place November to March is alleged neither free nor fair. All devices imaginable are used by the ruling regional parties to eliminate opponents. North–South tensions are exacerbated with violence between ethnic groups.

1966

January: Sir Abubakar Balewa and several other northern political and religious leaders are killed in a southern-led army coup d'état headed by Major Nzeogwu. The declared aim is to establish a strong, unified and prosperous nation, free from corruption and internal strife. Within days Major-General Johnson Aguiyi-Ironsi forms a new military government staffed mainly by southern officers and with only a token number of Muslim northerners.

May: Riots occur throughout northern Nigeria during which many easterners residing in the North are attacked and killed.

July: A counter-coup is staged by northern military officers on 29 July with two aims: revenge on the East for the earlier murders of traditional leaders and a break-up of the Nigerian Federation of States. In the process General Ironsi is killed and replaced by Lieutenant-Colonel Yakubu Gowon, a Christian and trusted officer from the country's central regions.

August: Troops of eastern Nigerian origin serving elsewhere in the country are offi-
              cially and formally released and posted to Enugu, the capital of the Eastern
              Region, while troops of non-eastern origin in Enugu are moved to Kaduna
              in the north and Lagos in the west. This marks the beginning of division
              and disunity within the rank and file of the Nigerian armed forces.

September: Senseless looting and killing spread throughout northern Nigeria, with tens
              of thousands of southerners—mainly from the Eastern Region—indiscrim-
              inately slaughtered. The majority of easterners—those who still can—flee
              to their tribal homeland.

October: Lieutenant-Colonel Odumegwu Ojukwu, commander of Nigeria's Eastern
              Region—who played no part in either of the military coups—broadcasts
              from Enugu that if the killings are not halted, he will be forced to take steps
              to stop the violence.

1967

January: Following a virulent war of words between the East and the North, peace
              talks between the Supreme Military Council of the Federal Republic of
              Nigeria and the country's Eastern Region are held under the auspices of
              Ghana's head of state, General Ankrah, in Aburi, Ghana. Nothing comes of
              the talks in spite of efforts at reconciliation by eminent Nigerians, Emperor
              Hallie Selassie of Ethiopia and Dr Martin Luther King.

May: The Nigerian Federal government divides the country into twelve states
              on 27 May 1967, with the Eastern Region subdivided into three states; the
              promulgation is rejected out of hand by Ojukwu.

June: Ojukwu seizes Federal government property and funds in the East. He
              plans the hijacking of a national commercial aircraft, a Fokker F27, on a
              scheduled flight from Benin to Lagos. All these and other indications—
              together with a succession of intelligence reports—convince the Federal
              Military Government of Ojukwu's intention to secede. Colonel Yakubu
              Gowon, the head of the Federal government imposes a total blockade of the
              East. By now both adversaries have started preparing for war.

July: Hostilities erupt on 6 July as the southeastern regions of Nigeria secede as
              the Republic of Biafra, sparking a bloody civil war that is to last three years.

July 1967–January 1970

The war that followed was a savage and often brutal battle for dominance between Federal
forces—supported by Britain and the Soviet Union (obviously the oil that lay under Biafran

earth had a lot to do with that unlikely alliance)—and a tiny enclave that was soon completely surrounded by its enemies. Much of what took place during almost three years of bitter fighting is both confused and puzzling because it all happened in a comparatively small region where travel was perilous because of Nigerian jet fighters hitting anything that moved on the roads. Also, the front could often move three or four times in a single day.

Accurate reports of what actually went on between the warring parties were invariably sketchy for several reasons, the first being heavy levels of censorship imposed on all news reports (and access) pushed out by news hacks and independent observers by the Lagos government. In contrast, that did not happen that often with Biafran events because, simply put, there was nobody there to report on it. None of this author's reports or scores of photographs were ever censored by Ojukwu's representatives.

Nigeria's restrictions were severe. For instance, the MiniCon rocket attack on the merchant ship *Titania*—on which I was travelling and which was hit by rocket fire while moored in the Warri roadstead—never made news. I wrote my report, hired a boat to take me into Warri town, and submitted the story to be telegraphed to the *Daily Express* in London (for which I paid a bundle); it was spiked by Federal goons. My editors never saw it. More salient, actual sequences of events, battles, attacks and the rest sometimes made little sense because both the Federals and Ojukwu's people channelled everything to do with hostilities through their respective public relations people, the latter in Geneva. The truth is that both would do their best to either obfuscate what actually happened or embellish it. That made nonsense of some events which would simultaneously appear the next morning in competing newspapers—the *Times* or the London *Daily Mail*, for instance— and might indeed have happened on different continents the way they were presented.

1970

10 January:	Ojukwu, on realizing the total chaotic hopelessness of the situation, hands over power to the commander of the Biafran army, Major-General Phillip Efiong, and flies out of the enclave with his immediate family to exile in the Ivory Coast.
14 January:	The Biafran surrender is signed four days later in Lagos.
1982:	In June, after thirteen years in exile, the Federal government of Nigeria under President Shagari, grants an official pardon to Odumegwu Ojukwu and opens the road for his triumphant return to eastern Nigeria. The people of Nnewi award him the famous chieftaincy title of *Ikemba* (Strength of the Nation).
1983:	In October a new military government takes over the country and arrests Ojukwu, subjecting him to close confinement in Lagos's notorious maximum security Kirikiri Prison.

A *durbar* of northern leaders at Nigerian independence.

1984:   In October, having not been charged with any crime, he is uncondi-
tionally released from detention and continues to play a major role in
regional politics. He is particularly outspoken about tribal killings of
easterners by northern factions that continue to this day.

1994:   In January Ojukwu marries Bianca Onoh, a former Miss Nigeria and
Nigeria's ambassador to Spain.

2011:   In November, after a brief illness, Ojukwu dies in the UK aged 78.

2012:   On 27 February the Nigerian army accords the former Biafran leader the
highest military accolade and conducts a funeral parade for him in the
Nigerian capital of Abuja, his body having been flown home from Britain
a short while before.

INTRODUCTION

We live in interesting times, no less so in Nigeria, Africa's most populous nation with an estimated 190 million people living there. There is no dispute as to whether Lagos, Nigeria's former capital, is Africa's most populous city, but the question today is, how big is it? Cairo held that claim for decades but the astonishingly fecund Nigerians have been catching up fast. When I lived in Lagos in the mid-1960s, we were told that our neighbours numbered about three or four million. By 2010 the figure was 'thought' to be about 12 million: nobody could be sure. These days the United Nations puts the population of that enormous under-nourished mega-metropolis at about 14 million but Lagos State Government maintains

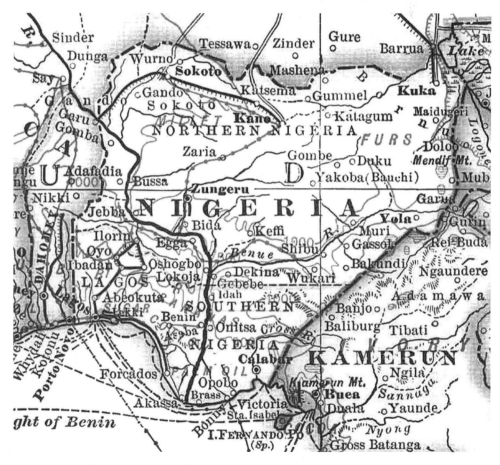

A 1909 National Geographic map of Nigeria.

that it could be closer to the mark with a total of 21 million. Go on like that say the doom merchants and it could easily top 45 or 50 million by 2050, sixty percent under the age of twenty-five. And that's a not much more than a generation away.

Nigeria has a rather interesting history, which tends to be ignored these days because it is linked to the colonial period and the average Nigerian does not like to be reminded that until 1960 his country was ruled from London. Lagos was captured by British forces in 1851 and formally annexed in 1861. It took another forty years and several invasions into the interior for the country to be made a British protectorate. That was in 1901 and imperial rule lasted less than six decades.

Even then, Nigeria was 'split' between the Islamic North and the mostly Christian or 'animist' South, administered directly by an army of colonial functionaries whose principal measure of control beyond city limits was the DC, or district commissioner. The idea caught on and there were soon DCs in every other British colony north of the Limpopo as well.

In northern Nigeria it was emirs and Sardaunas who held sway and the entire region was left to its own devices under the appropriately named 'Indirect Rule', initiated by the that arch-imperialist Frederick Lugard, First Baron Lugard, or as we know him today, Lord Lugard, founder of the West African Frontier Force.

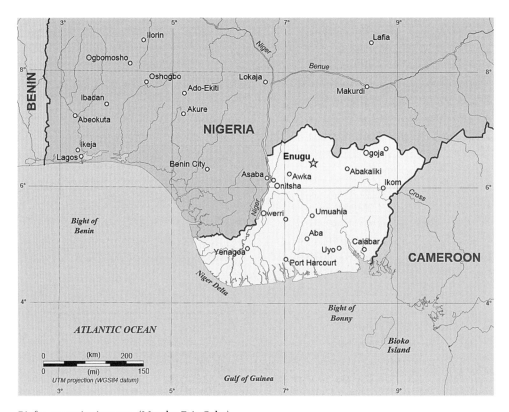

Biafra, secessionist state. (Map by Eric Gaba)

It was notable that he maintained the DC presence in the north and these young British 'upstarts', as the Nigerians sometimes liked to call them, were a feature of the colonial administration, though they invariably yielded to traditional northern authority when requested to do so.

The colonial period was remarkable for the progress the country achieved in infra-structure—schools, clinics, hospitals, administrative centres and rail links—with, it seemed, the entire nation pulling together. If India was the 'Jewel in the British Crown', Nigeria—as one London wag on assignment in that part of the world once declared—was its 'African Pearl'.

I travelled through the country the first time in 1965, only five years after independence and I discovered a remarkably vibrant, friendly community whose enthusiasm was, if any-thing, infectious. First impressions were of a really delightful former colony, so much so that when I tired of British strikes and London weather not long afterward, I applied for a job with John Holt, one of the original 'Coaster' firms in the country and got it. The appel-lation refers to 'old coasters', colonial types who had been living along the West African seaboard almost forever, many of whom had 'gone bush'. The Gold Coast (Ghana after independence) had its 'coasters', so did Sierra Leone, the Gambia and, of course, Nigeria.

I regarded my posting to Nigeria in January 1966 as a quite remarkable gift and could not wait to get back to Africa, the only problem being that a few days before my plane touched down at Ikeja International Airport, elements within the Nigerian Army staged a coup d'état. In the process some army officers murdered a string of Nigerian politicians, religious leaders as well as more than a few of their commanders.

One of the first to be murdered by the rebellious soldiers was the highly respected Alhaji Sir Abubakar Tafawa Balewa, not only a revered leader of the country's Islamic community but also the first prime minister of an independent Nigeria. He had been knighted a few years before by Queen Elizabeth II as a Knight Commander of the Order of the British Empire and, coincidentally, was also awarded an honorary doctorate from the University of Sheffield.

Another notable cut down was Sir Abubakar's old companion, Ahmadou Bello, the only premier of the northern Nigerian region who also held the title of Sardauna of Sokoto, regarded as top ranking in Africa's lofty Islamic climes.

The circumstances surrounding Bello's death still remain unresolved, except that it was brutal. His body was discovered at a roadside near Lagos six days after he had been taken from his office. News of his assassination spurred riots throughout northern Nigeria and ultimately led to the bloody counter-coup of July 1966, launched ironically from the same Ikeja International Airport where I had my office. That event ultimately led to the Biafran war. In the lead-up to hostilities, an awful number of southern people died, the majority from the Nigerian Ibo tribe regarded by recalcitrant Islamic northerners as the prime architects of the January slaughters. In the process, the Nigerian civil war started in 1967 and ended thirty months later, one of the first times Western consciences were awakened and deeply affronted by the level of the suffering and the scale of the atrocities played out in this corner of the African continent.

Sir Abubakar Tafawa
Balewa.

As Chinua Achebe is recorded as saying once the country was plunged into bloody
turmoil, "The only thing we have learnt from experience is that we learn nothing from
experience," an expression that aptly describes Nigeria's fruitless toil to make headway
politically, economically and technologically once first blood had been spilled.

Essentially, this book is about many of the events which followed that first violent oust-
ing of a Nigerian government by the army in January 1966 and, until the Boko Haram
Insurgency in the north, it was Nigeria's longest and bloodiest conflict.

Some of what took place can be gleaned from an internal briefing held by Washington's
National Security Agency after hostilities had broken out on 6 July 1967, now declassified.
The war cost roughly a million lives (of which only a modest proportion were fighting
men) and ended abruptly on 15 January 1970 after the rebels had been eventually starved
into submission. The NSA briefing was brief and to the point. It dealt first with an over-
view of civil war:

The Nigerian Federation united three major ethnic groups and about 250 smaller
ones. From British colonial tutelage, it developed a reasonably workable political
cohesion and decidedly promising economic prospects through five years of independence. But the corruption and indecisiveness of first generation politicians
triggered a coup in 1966 by young army officers, mostly Ibos from eastern Nigeria.

The tribal implications of that coup triggered in turn a sequence of assassinations,
tribal atrocities and polarization culminating in eastern Nigeria's secession as 'Biafra'
and the outbreak. The war [quickly] stalemated with Federal Military Government
troops surrounding a 7,000 square mile Biafran enclave, or about a quarter of the
30,000 square miles the rebels began with and containing five to seven million people.

Despite Federal military superiority in men and materiel, there is very little prospect that either side by itself can win militarily ... unless Biafra's arms supply is cut off. The two sides are fighting a total war and subordinate humanitarian to political objectives. Moreover, mutual tribal enmities complicate and embitter the political issues.

A Biafran propaganda poster. (Author's photo)

It went on to explain that about the two million people left in Biafra after the enclave had been 'squeezed' by Federal forces depended absolutely on nighttime airlifts operated by several religious voluntary agencies that were operating from the Portuguese island of São Tomé and by the International Committee of the Red Cross (ICRC) from Dahomey (Benin today). More flights came from Libreville in former French Gabon (mainly arms, with starving children brought back on the return flight to be tended by French and interdenominational religious and welfare groups) and to a lesser extent Dahomey and former Spanish Guinea.

Every war has its cathartic moments for those who are involved and Biafra was no exception. To my mind—and I have covered quite a few conflicts, revolts, army mutinies and revolutions—it was also very different from all the other wars I've witnessed from up close: sometimes too close, which is why I am almost deaf. In my case, this West African conflict was a life-changing experience that I never quite got over: for several reasons.

I'd arrived in Lagos very soon after the first army mutiny had taken place. Though my office was at Ikeja airport and I should have been aware of what was taking place in my own 'backyard', I was as surprised as the next man when I discovered that Ikeja was where the second revolution had been planned and executed by a small group of army officers who had nothing in common, tribally or otherwise.

The only difference with the second army mutiny was that it was mainly soldiers from Nigeria's Islamic North in the driving seat—and they were almost all Muslims. As the phrase suggests, it was 'payback time'.

The first place targeted the second time round was Ikeja airport, followed by attacks on the headquarters of the Nigerian police, State House, naval headquarters at Apapa,

Harold Wilson, the British prime minister who, because of strategic oil reserves, took the UK into the war allied with the Soviets in support of Federal Nigeria.

as well as the offices of the national radio station. Other government civilian and military agencies and installations were taken over soon afterward.

One of my early chapters details the bloody battle in the vicinity of Lagos's international airport, a singular event which set off a chain of events that resulted in the civil war. I was on my way to work and inadvertently I stumbled into the aftermath of that bloody early-morning firefight that involved dissident army units and armour. The battle for Ikeja lasted less than an hour and was the brainchild of Lieutenant-Colonel Murtala Muhammed, after whom the airport was subsequently renamed, but who was himself assassinated a year after taking over as Nigeria's military ruler in 1975.

It is worth mentioning that prior to the second army mutiny my job entailed a considerable amount of travel throughout Nigeria. During the course of those duties I met a lot of people, both in civilian and government roles, including quite a few military types in the various hotels and bars along the way. In those early days everybody could freely express their opinions because the all-encompassing security apparatus for which Nigeria became notorious in subsequent military governments only came later. British author Frederick Forsyth told me when we got together at my home in Washington State thirty years later, that he still didn't dare visit the country: "I'm pretty sure they would kill me if I did," were his words.

Following the first revolution, it did not take much gumption to appreciate that there were some serious things taking place, both in Lagos and in northern Nigeria. Travelling about the country as I did, I could actually sense that another revolution was imminent. I even predicted as much in several magazines for which I was writing at the time, including the now-defunct *News Check* as well as the mass-circulation *Huisgenoot*, both published in South Africa. It is all on file for those interested in looking back on those almost forgotten chapters of Africa's post-independence history. I was also doing the odd story for United Press International in London at the time, but their editors scoffed at the premise that more Nigerian violence might follow the first army coup. So, apparently, did Britain's intelligence agencies. Like Washington, they were, as the saying goes, caught with their pants around their ankles when it happened.

Prior to that, when I started reporting back my fears of another possible army revolt to my bosses at John Holt, they were appalled. It took no time at all for the order to come down from the top: instead of meddling in political matters, you should concentrate on your work, or something similar, was the gist of it. But then, when it happened at midnight on 29 July 1966, even the British high commission in Lagos was found seriously wanting: they were clueless.

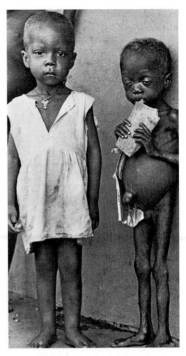

Victims of the Biafran War ... mostly children.

Looking back at those events and my subsequently going into Biafra itself—my first real experience of a war—it might be trite to say that I was severely affected by the plight of thousands of emaciated and starving children encountered at every turn in the beleaguered state: I was, rather severely so, and I don't believe I ever got over it.

Three decades later, while covering the civil war in Sierra Leone, I spent some time at the Murraytown amputee camp on the outskirts of Freetown and that same horrifically emotional experience haunted me for months, something I go into in some detail in one of my earlier books about that country's insurrection: *War Dog: Fighting Other People's Wars*

Biafra had the immediate effect of changing my approach to what was going on in Africa at the time, South Africa included. It would be banal to say that what I discovered in Biafra was unsettling in the extreme. But it was. The majority of kids—by then, mostly orphaned—were gathered together in camps run by the various aid groups and given whatever assistance could be made available. Inside a beleaguered Biafra, there wasn't much. When I got there, it was clear to just about all of us that the 'air bridge' from São Tomé, Fernando Pó, Libreville and elsewhere was simply not bringing in enough food to feed everybody. Biafra was fighting a war and many of the planes arriving after dark were stacked with ammunition. As a result, most of those who died in that war either starved to death or were so debilitated that their frail bodies were unable to counter infection or disease. I would imagine that following Hitler's death camps, it was a severe case of *déjà vu*.

Left: Lieutenant-Colonel Chukwuemeka Odumegwu Ojukwu takes the salute.

Below: Lieutenant-Colonel Yakubu Gowon heads the Nigerian delegation at an OAU summit.

This 1968 photograph shows a major road intersection where refugees of the civil war would congregate in order to receive food distributions during relief efforts during the late 1960s. (Photo CDC/ Dr Lyle Conrad\)

It is also true that conditions in the rebel enclave were exacerbated by the constantly changing fortunes of war: the front line would alternately bulge or contract, sometimes quite dramatically and often overnight as one side or the other gained a tactical advantage. With time, areas dominated by Colonel Chukwuemeka Odumegwu Ojukwu's rebel command steadily diminished, and that went on until all his big towns were lost. Then it was only a matter of time. I stayed on in the rebel territory until the last few weeks and by then it was pretty obvious to us all that when it came, the collapse would be quick. It was, and Ojukwu got out on the second-last flight.

Frederick Forsyth, who had been there almost from the start, also cut it fine, because when I departed, he had been hospitalized with malaria. I'd intended to bid my farewell, but travelling on Biafra's roads by then—with the skies dominated by Nigerian fighter aircraft that regarded anything on the ground as fair game—I accepted the quick offer of a flight to Libreville. That meant I did not dither when I was told to get myself to Uli airport. At that late stage, if you had a seat you took it because the planes were on the ground for perhaps thirty minutes. Then they were off again. The aircrews simply did not wait landbound to be bombed by the Nigerian air force's foreign-crewed DC-3, appropriately dubbed 'Marauder', and when the mood took it, 'Genocide'.

1. THE BIAFRAN WAR

Until the Boko Haram insurgency, Nigeria's longest and bloodiest conflict was its civil war. Its origins were to be found in numerous issues that plagued this former British colony at the time, almost all subtly bubbling, unseen, just below the surface. Apart from some serious ethnic differences and a scheming military, there was government corruption at an apocalyptic level. Finally, when push came to shove, the secession of the southeastern provinces of Nigeria followed and in the process many people died. For all that, I was to find in Nigeria a wonderfully exuberant and friendly country the first time I set foot there in 1965. Indeed, the Nigeria of January 1966—a bit more than eighteen months later—was a very different place from the one I encountered while hiking up the west coast of Africa to get to London.

When I first visited the place I was overwhelmed by a plethora of first impressions, in large part because my native South Africa was never like this. Initial notions were of an effervescent *joie de vivre* that seemed to infect all levels of society and a very realistic hope that would ultimately deliver to the world Black Africa's leading nation.

I'd originally entered Nigeria by dugout canoe from the Cameroons, spent a few days in a magic little backwater called Calabar and paid my way in bush taxis and mammy wagons through Port Harcourt, Onitsha and Benin all the way to Lagos, where I promptly went down with malaria.

I wasn't down for long, and once on my feet again I continued with a rather personal discovery of Africa's most lively country.

The prime minister of Northern Nigeria, Ahmadou Bello, inspects a traditional guard of honour on his visit to Raba.

Wherever this white boy from apartheid-infused South Africa went into what was then a federation of Nigerian states, I was feted, fed and displayed to everybody who was curious to know what somebody from the 'Racist South' was like. Even my skin and hair were touched by some to make sure I was real; others, in efforts to uncover whatever thoughts about race or African people I might have secreted, plied me with enough Star beer to set up a roadside stall. And when that did not work, they tried palm wine. Throughout, I never once encountered any hostility, political or otherwise. Indeed, Lagos in those distant days was among the most amicable and secure cities on the continent.

We were out just about every night, mostly on foot moving around the bars and clubs on Victoria Island or up Ikorodu road, often till the wee hours: a mugging in those days was about as alien to the average Nigerian as flush toilets in their impecunious wooden and tin-can homes.

What then went wrong? What was it that thrust this remarkable showpiece former colony into one of the most horrific civil wars that Africa was to experience for the next half century?

More damnable, hostilities kicked off only two or three years after my first visit and that cataclysm changed Nigeria forever. No corner of the country was left untouched. There have been numerous theories about Nigeria's social, political and military break-down that went on to foment two army mutinies which eventually led to war.

The first of these is historical and goes back to the early colonial epoch. Essentially, it boils down to the reality that Nigeria was too big and disparate to administer as a single unified

With Bible in hand, Colonel Odumegwu Ojukwu declares Biafra's secession from the Federal government, May 1967.

state. Put another way, there were simply too many irreconcilable forces pulling in different directions. On the one hand you had an enormous Islamic society in the north, numbering tens of millions, and on the other, a very different set of circumstances in the south.

Much of Nigeria along its seaboard—from the Cameroons to Dahomey (Benin)—was mainly Christian and animist, usually suffused with good dollops of juju to even out the divine laws of probability. And let it be said: that is not supposition or hearsay; it is the reality of everyday life in much of Africa today. Unlike the Islamic people of the north who had always been regarded with almost undisguised disdain by the majority of southerners, the big cities of the south quickly transmogrified into fast-moving commercial and industrial hubs where nothing mattered except the money on the table.

Nigeria's original foundation as a country had a lot to do with the political outcome that became pronounced in 1966, and much of that was based on conquest by British forces almost a century before. Originally created by Britain when Nigeria became a protectorate, this enormous country—roughly three times the size of either Germany or Italy—was figuratively split down the middle between competing factions.

Also, the south was plagued by a history of grudges—transmitted verbally over centuries from one generation to the next. Its essence was that it was the dusky Moorish and Arab people from the north—allied to the Hausas and the Fulanis—who had helped European adventurers to foster the slave trade. And while that iniquity happened a long time ago, its reality and its consequences is carved almost indelibly in the mind of the average southern psyche.

Biafran soldiers in Asaba.

Religion followed, which, in the African context can include staunch Roman Catholic or Islamic clerics sharing the same sidewalk as the local voodoo soothsayer, or perhaps a minaret within muezzin-calling-distance of the local cathedral. But none of this mattered in the colonial days because under British rule everybody lived comfortably, unblinkingly accepting the unfettered beliefs and social mores of others.

Following independence in 1960, three provinces were formed along tribal lines. These were composed of the Hausa and Fulani in the north, the Yoruba in the southwest and Igbo or, more commonly before and during the conflict, the Ibo nation toward the southeast.

And then, to the surprise of all, civil war erupted only seven years later, which suggests either an extremely shallow set of underpinning political guidelines or something intrinsically wrong with the original concept of self-determination.

It is notable that France gave almost all its African colonies their independence at about the same time as Nigeria, and for decades they were spared the kind of turmoil that spawned Biafra. One significant reason surfaces almost immediately. The French went about their imperial business very differently. Instead of creating one or more immense mega-countries like Nigeria across its equatorial fief that stretched two-thirds the way across the continent, Paris carved up its colonies into easily identifiable entities, the majority based on old established regions as well as tribal affinities. Britain, in contrast, chose to keep Nigeria 'intact': a vast country that stretched from the tropical Atlantic coast to the periphery of the sub-Saharan Sahel and contained hundreds of different groups. Then, without reference to anybody, least of all those living there, they 'unified' it all and though there was one central government authority in Lagos, each region enjoyed a solid measure of autonomy, the north especially.

In the southern portions of the country, regional governments emulated the British system, but the semi-feudal Islamic North took a decidedly different route. Their citizens were traditionally ruled by an autocratic and conservative Islamic hierarchy that consisted of 30-odd emirs who, in turn, owed their allegiance to a supreme sultan.

This 'supremo' was regarded as the source of all political power and religious authority and obviously, when a crazy bunch of southern soldiers murdered some of their leaders, there were bound to be consequences.

It was the Nigerian army mutiny—a full-blown coup d'état launched on the night of 15 January 1966—that changed everything. A group of young officers, led by left-leaning Major Chukwuma Nzeogwu—apparently frustrated with the political situation—planned and executed a coup with a small group of like-minded ideologists that went on to overthrow the Federal government. In the process

'Jack' Gowon looking relaxed.

two regional premiers, a prime minister, eight other politicians and two of his own officers, considered to be too closely linked to the north or opposed to the takeover, died violently.

In retrospect, it did not appear that the plotters had anything resembling a coherent post-army mutiny plan beyond eliminating those politicians whom they believed wielded too much power. Their dreadful deeds done, the dissidents were eventually persuaded to surrender by the most senior surviving officer, Major-General Aguiyi Ironsi who formed a Federal military government and replaced former premiers with military officers.

What also emerged rather sharply was that the majority of those involved with the killings were from Nigeria's Eastern Region.

Historically, West Africa is somewhat different from most other regions of the world and while the initial reaction to the murders within the upper echelons was muted, northern Nigeria was appalled. Their beloved leaders had been cut down and, in traditional African fashion, they said very little. They waited and planned very carefully before responding.

What did take place almost immediately though, was that the murders spilled over into several widespread pogroms—particularly in the northern and central parts of the country—against people who were of eastern origin, some of whom had been living in the north for generations. One and all, they were sought out and killed—men, women and children—which led to an estimated 30,000 deaths within the first few months of the 'many nights of the long knives' as some described the atrocities.

The Biafran chief of staff, Major-General Philip Efiong.

Because of the violence—most times mindless and unbridled—which soon became constant, it also resulted in a large-scale displacement of Ibos and other easterners back to the Eastern Region. Negotiations to resolve this crisis between the new head of the Federal Military Government (FMG), Lieutenant-Colonel Yakubu Gowon and the governor of the Eastern Region, Lieutenant-Colonel Odumegwu Ojukwu, broke down almost from the start.

It was then that Ojukwu warned Gowon—and the nation as a whole in a series of radio broadcasts—that if the killings continued, he would take his people out of the Nigerian Federation.

Meanwhile, pogroms against easterners in the north of the country continued unabated and seemingly with a new intensity. On the face of it there seemed to be no way to resolve this impasse. The end result was that Ojukwu unilaterally declared his Eastern Region independent and proclaimed the establishment of the Republic of Biafra.

That single act signalled the start of the civil war.

Opposing Forces

Nigeria

GROUND: The Nigerian army had a small professional force of 10,500 men, descended from the Royal West African Frontier Force. Two brigades were organized into six Infantry battalions, there were two batteries of 105mm guns as well as a pair of armoured car reconnaissance squadrons. Additionally there was also a solid, professional back-up with engineer, signals and other service troops.

The national army, originally under British guidance, was recruited from a population of an estimated 60 million people. It ended the war with an army of more than 100,000 troops divided into three divisions, and more than the normal complement of brigades. The chaos originating from the army mutinies and, of necessity, extremely rapid expansion meant that the Federal force was hampered by poor leadership, coordination and administration.

It should be mentioned that prior to the civil war, recruitment in the Nigerian armed forces was heavily in favour of the south. When the country gained its independence from Britain in 1960, roughly fifteen percent of Nigeria's military officer corps came from the north and the west. Most of those who replaced white British officers were of Ibo or eastern extraction. To avoid friction between the three regions, London was obliged to determine that the army should be recruited by quota, and if ever there was a recipe for disaster, this was it.

As we have seen many times over the past, quotas have never worked on a continent dominated by hidden agendas, especially where tribe and ethnicity are factors. In theory, under the new arrangement, 50 percent of all officers were to come from the north, with the east and the west splitting the balance between them. By the time the first army mutiny took place in January 1966, Ibos still filled about half the places that Britain offered to Nigeria at Sandhurst.

Once again, in the eyes of their adversaries—particularly those in the north—the crafty Ibo had shown that he was pushier than the rest. Some Nigerians regarded the fact that easterners seemed to be taking over the Federal army as dangerous, positively so, and ran editorials in some of the northern newspapers.

As Frederick Forsyth wrote—he spent a lot of time in Biafra and wrote a classic book on the war, *Biafra Story: The Making of an African Legend*—"it was also clear from the start that the Nigerian army was a rabble, a shambles from beginning to end."

Government forces did get their act together after a while, mainly because they either did so or they went down. Yakubu Gowon then proceeded to blockade all Biafra's ports and within months the conflict had degenerated into one of the most brutal tit-for-tat wars of attrition Africa has seen since the end of World War II.

Fighting everywhere was vicious. In many instances, it was totally confused. Towns changed hands, sometimes three or four times within weeks. Eventually the preponderance

Biafran front-line casualties were manhandled away from the combat zone, more often than not at night.

of Federal power prevailed and the Biafrans were pushed back, first from the coast and finally into several loosely linked enclaves in the heavily forested interior. Very early on already, atrocities at the hands of what had become a northern-dominated, mainly Islamic force soon convinced the rebel nation that secession from Federation was no longer the principal issue. Rather, it had become an all-out battle for survival.

AIR: the fledgling air force was being trained by the West German Luftwaffe when the war broke out and many pilots and technicians were easterners who returned home. The Nigerian air force eventually consisted of MiG-17 and MiG-15 fighter bombers, Tupolev medium bombers and Czech Delphin L-29 strike aircraft.

At the start of the war most of these aircraft were flown by Egyptians, but within a comparatively short time mercenary pilots were recruited abroad and they took over most day-to-day operational roles while Nigerians were being trained. The Egyptian pilots, by then, had become notorious for their incompetence and inability to get to grips with the problem, which meant that foreign mercenary pilots controlled the war in the air to the end of hostilities.

SEA: the Nigerian navy consisted of a frigate and several patrol boats at the start of hostilities. Though it took time, these ships mounted an effective blockade of the Biafran coast, which prevented just about all heavy shipping from accessing rebel landing sites. Quite a lot of smaller shipping did manage to breach the blockade.

Biafra

GROUND: The Biafran army started off with a single combat unit, the 1st Battalion, Biafran Army (formerly 1st Battalion, Nigerian Army, Enugu) in 1967. The Biafran army eventually grew to seven divisions and many brigades, though the majority, because of manpower problems, operated well below full strength. Throughout, the Biafran army was in no way comparable in strength, firepower or manpower to what Lagos's central authority was able to put into the field.

AIR: the Biafrans were the first to launch a fully functioning air force and were also the first to conduct airstrikes. This situation was rapidly reversed with the arrival of Soviet MiGs, mercenaries and the loss of the Port Harcourt and Enugu airfields. A brief resurgence was seen with the use of armed Swedish-built MiniCon trainer aircraft—the

MFI-9B MiniCoin, corrupted to MiniCon—flown both by easterners who had previously served in the Nigerian air force, unpaid European volunteers as well as a small squad of mercenaries. These planes, soon joined by surplus American Texan AT-6s and some antiquated World War II bombers, were effectively deployed against strategic Nigerian targets such as airfields, shipping and logistics bases.

I was caught up in one of these attacks while on board the Scandinavian freighter *Titania*, moored in the roadstead in the Niger Delta port of Warri. We took hits from several rockets and had a few injuries but nothing serious. Not so the Farrell Line ship berthed ahead of us that had two crew members killed.

NAVY: the Biafran navy consisted of a Nigerian navy gunboat and other vessels captured in the early days and converted by Ojukwu's people. After initial battles along the Rivers coastline—which the secessionists eventually lost—the Biafran navy resorted to mine warfare, using locally constructed mines along the navigable routes to Port Harcourt. The Biafran navy ceased to exist as a maritime fighting force after the fall of Port Harcourt and Calabar, save for isolated sorties around Oguta and other strongpoints in the Niger Delta.

The War

In the aftermath of initial mobilization, the Federal army attacked from the south, mounting a riverine campaign, via Bonny, in an effort to capture Port Harcourt, the second biggest city in Biafra with a port, airport, refinery and power station. At the same time,

Biafran troops preparing 'Ojukwu buckets'—homemade claymore mines—for ambush. (Author's photo)

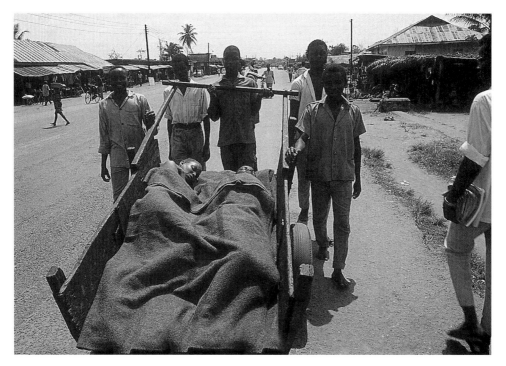

Biafran wounded being taken to a clinic in a makeshift ambulance. (Author's photo)

the Federals attempted to open a new front to the east of Biafra by attacking from Asaba into the direction of Onitsha, which was repulsed repeatedly with heavy losses.

Onitsha was eventually taken, but from another direction, though the Federal 2nd Division never fully recovered from it losses. In the south, Port Harcourt and Calabar were taken, completely isolating the rebel enclave from the world outside.

Inexorably, the war for the Federal forces became a slow and extremely tedious advance inland, with the operational cycle consisting of major Federal offensives during the dry season and Biafran counteroffensives when the rains came as they retreated into the rain forests of the Ibo heartland.

The end came when a tiny sliver of land around the strategic Uli airport—formerly a section of the main road between Aba and Onitsha—was all that was left as Biafra came under concerted attack from all sides in a final offensive in December 1969. That led to the collapse of Ojukwu's starving army, a ceasefire and finally, surrender.

The Biafran war, in its day, generated several significant issues: Why did Biafra lose and could Ojukwu possibly have achieved victory if the war went on long enough? All these issues are dealt with in more detail in subsequent chapters.

At the end of the war, Lieutenant-Colonel Gowon declared, publically and emphatically, that there would be, as he phrased it, "No victor and no vanquished." Additionally, there

During the civil war, many Nigerian schools, like the one, were used as clinics or food distribution points for refugees. (Photo CDC/ Dr. Lyle Conrad)

were no show trials, no summary executions or arguably any more mayhem than might have been expected under the circumstances.

Certainly, there were excesses, but none of these were organized: they were mainly mood-of-the-moment indulgences, usually as a consequence of too much liquor and too little thought of the consequences.

To its credit, the Federal Military Government did set about organizing fairly substantial relief and reconstruction programmes for the vanquished and, after a period of assessment as to what would be best for the country, Biafra was split into three: East Central, Rivers and the Cross Rivers states of Nigeria.[*]

---

[*] Information for this chapter has been drawn from Open Source Intelligence, Vox Peccavi: West African Security & Risk Management, as well as from the author's personal experiences in Nigeria and in Biafra before, during and after the war.

2. THAT MEMORABLE FIRST MORNING OF FIGHTING IN LAGOS

It all happened so unexpectedly. On the morning of 19 July 1966 I was in my car driving to work from my apartment in Apapa, a Lagos suburb, when I suddenly found myself in the middle of what had been—perhaps twenty minutes before—a bloody battle. I had just turned off the main road to the airport when I saw bodies—dozens of them—strewn along the roadside. Nigerian army troop-carriers and civilian vehicles, some burning, one or two capsized and others abandoned lay all over the place. There were also a lot of dead and wounded.

My immediate problem at that moment was that I had already made a terrible mistake by turning off the main highway and into the road that led to my office at Ikeja airport. I did not know it yet, but effectively I was directly in the line of fire of a squad of troops that had obviously initiated this battle. Fortunately, the shooting had stopped. I could, of course, have tried to reverse onto the highway, but that would have drawn attention and, possibly, something worse. So I did the only thing left: I drove slowly and deliberately ahead toward the main airport compound, as I had done just about every morning since I'd arrived in the country. In spite of the carnage round me, I acted as if it were all a familiar daily occurrence. My radio was on, my elbow rested on the open window and I tapped on the wheel in time to a high-life tune. I twisted my face into what I hoped would be interpreted as a smile. What else to do?

Then, quite bewildering, for I hadn't seen another soul—apart from the casualties scattered about—there they were: half a dozen soldiers prostrate on the ground gathered around a couple of heavy machine guns. I had no idea what kind they were but the weapons did look pretty formidable from where I was perched at the wheel of my Ford and every barrel was pointed in my direction.

Al Venter (right) with Tony Cusack from Liverpool (left) with a Nigerian colleague while working for John Holt in Lagos. (Author's collection)

Worse, I had to go right past them before I could finally turn toward the airport. Their position was at the side of the road and I suppose I could have ridden over them if I had been crazy enough to do so.

Once abreast of the soldiers I lifted a hand and waved. "Good morning, gentlemen," I called loudly, still smiling. "Everything okay?" I drove on and kept waving because nobody ordered me to stop ... the troops manning the guns certainly did not respond. All were grim-faced and silent, which I thought at the time was really not a good sign. I suppose they were as nonplussed as I was: my sudden appearance on the road leading to the airport obviously didn't quite fall within the scope of their orders which would have been something along the lines of kill anybody that approaches, exactly as they had cut down those in the convoy that had preceded me a short while before.

I was aware, of course, that there had been plenty of killings during the troubles in the months after I had arrived in Nigeria. There had actually been some people shot at Ikeja a few weeks before, but even though we asked the local police what had happened, no one was volunteering anything.

The Ikeja road attack was obviously different: one squad of soldiers in vehicles and some armour had been ambushed by an opposing squad lying in wait under the clumps of bushes I had just driven past. My initial impression, confirmed informally later that morning by one of the officers I spoke to outside my John Holt office at the airport, was that this had been a regular pitched battle and those youngsters that I had seen—none could have been out of their teens—had been responsible.

It was a stupid battle, he told me, deadly serious, "Shouldn't have happened."

The first thing I did when I finally got to the airport was call my boss at the main John Holt office in Apapa. He and the others were aware that I had gone to work that morning, but all the telephone lines were cut and they couldn't find out whether I was one of about

Ikeja airport, the Nigerian Air Force base; this photo was taken from the author's nearby office. (Author's photo)

29

twenty-odd people killed in the ambush on the Ikeja road. One of the dead was an expatriate, a Lebanese businessman caught in crossfire.

I took no chances on my return that evening. This time I got permission to go back through army lines to the main road that would take me toward the city. The officer in charge, a Hausa who had been to Sandhurst and loved it, escorted me and spoke fondly of the rugby he had watched at Twickenham as we drove. It was like that in West Africa in the old days.

By the time we reached that same stretch of road at about five o'clock that evening, all the bodies and wrecked vehicles that I'd seen there earlier on that day had been removed. Everything seemed peaceful once more. It would have been hard to believe that Nigerian soldiers were at that moment slaughtering every Ibo in the country who had not fled.

The Pax Britannica was only a memory. Africa was itself again. And let's face it, for those who know Africa's west coast, there are moments in Nigeria when things can be very deceptive.

The expatriate community—of which I had become a part in Lagos—was a mixed bunch. Many were there because they couldn't succeed elsewhere else. The Nigerians, by and large, were well aware of their shortcomings. These misfits—all of them in comfortable jobs arranged by somebody 'back home'—were known rather deprecatingly as 'white trash'. Looking back, I suppose some of them were. Their interests rarely extended beyond cheap Nigerian hooch and a never-ending array of dusky floozies.

Biafran troops at drill.

The majority were British, though there was a fair sprinkling of Australasians, Canadians and European nationals. There was even a South African technician at Ikeja airport, doing specialized work so the Nigerians let him stay; there was no other contact with the 'Racist South', except that the mail got through. Our status was dictated strictly by the given or implied terms of our contracts. Certainly, the 'tween-ranks pecking order was maintained by a system that smacked of militarism, a tradition that went back a century or more in this part of Africa in the erstwhile British and French colonies: officers simply did not mix with those from lower decks.

Yet, it was a good life. Accommodation—according to your status—came as part of the deal that you were offered before you left 'home'. It was always 'home', never Britain or England. Higher echelons got houses; those pathetic creatures lower down the scale, like me, were given apartments. All were rent free and included a steward, a rather appropriate euphemism for a servant in the former British colony. A manager could have three or four if he had children or entertained a lot. Many did. I had to settle for one, since he was paid for by the company. There was a complicated array of perks. For those who qualified, there were one or two or even more free flights home each year. Also, if you were lucky, the firm paid for your children's education at public schools in Britain. Their travel—two or three times a year between Heathrow and Lagos, Kano or one of the eastern 'stations'—was also part of the package.

The big expat event of the week in Lagos, Kano, Port Harcourt and elsewhere was the Sunday curry lunch at the club. It was a grand, boozy affair to which few locals were ever invited. In the old days the clubs had been fairly vigorously segregated along racial lines, even though there was nothing defined, no bylaws stipulating that blacks were not welcome: it was just the accepted thing. Nigerians had their own clubs anyway, it was argued. That changed quickly once the military took over. It simply had to. When a Nigerian soldier arrived at my 'local', the Apapa Club, and ordered a Star or a Guinness he was served with a smile. He wasn't even asked for money. Word quickly got around the barracks.

There were other distractions. The most important of these centred around the fact that in these outlying posts of what had once been Empire, there were few eligible females from back home. Those that were there worked in the embassies or with various aid or religious missions. Quite a few were Peace Corps or British VSO. There were, of course, many married women not averse to extramarital dalliances, but in a small, thoroughly integrated social environment like Lagos, such liaisons rarely lasted long before people started to talk. Indeed, it was difficult to have any kind of a clandestine life in the former colonies. Every one of us was under some kind of surveillance, if not from our bosses then from the government. As a result you either cooled your heels or you were sent home in disgrace.

There were any number of local girls, but in those days it was just not done to be seen with one on your arm in the club. Upcountry, yes, but not in your parlour, as it were; no ways. These things were happening, naturally, but always well away from expatriate residential areas. And anyway most of my associates did not advertise their predilection for 'something dark'. That came later in the evening at any one of hundreds of little open-air

Ikeja airport:
a British-made
Ferret armoured
car manned by
Nigerian troops.
(Author's photo)

clubs along Ikeja road, Yaba, Ebute-Metta or on Victoria Island. And those who did imbibe were discreet about it.

It was to the Apapa Club that I went on the morning after my escape at Ikeja. Obviously, nothing quite like that had ever happened before; the January army mutiny was a Wednesday afternoon exercise in the West Country by comparison. More ominous with the latest uprising was the fact that the Nigerian army was everywhere. The British high commission and other diplomatic missions encouraged a low profile for us all. Those not at work gathered at their respective clubs and compared notes, even though the stories did seem to improve with telling as the beer flowed.

By lunch on the second day, I decided to have a look at things for myself. Wilf Nussey, who ran the Argus Africa News Service out of the *Star* newspaper offices in Johannesburg, had been calling; he wanted to know what was happening. But because I did not have my usual easy access to Ikeja, I wasn't able to file in my usual manner. Certainly I did not have the facilities of Reuters, the BBC or any of the other news agencies based in Nigeria; I was still the backroom boy and, for the moment, that suited me fine.

Discussing it with my friends at the club, I decided that since the largest naval base in the country lay adjacent to Apapa docks, perhaps a kilometre from the club, I thought, I might possibly learn something by visiting the place. Why not? After all, the Nigerian navy was regarded as the most disciplined and best ordered of the Nigerian forces. Also, since I was living there, I had a rough idea of how to get to the base, even though the roads in the area were a mess. They had been laid over what had once been a swamp and followed no set grid pattern.

After a couple of wrong turns in the car, I eventually came to a road that led directly to the naval base; it lay dead ahead, about 500 metres away. Its steel gates were shut and the towers on either side, from what I could see at a distance, appeared to be manned. Certainly it looked ominous and I was unsure of what to do next. I had stopped in the middle of the road and that was another mistake.

While contemplating whether to go back or not, a siren sounded. The gates were thrown and a squad of about a dozen soldiers—all armed—rushed out. An officer appeared and called loudly: *"You there! You come here or we shoot! Now!"*

I hesitated a moment. Then a shot rang out. It was the officer, pistol in hand, firing in my direction. That basically decided it for me and I drove slowly ahead, again trying the pasted smile and elbow-on-the-window routine. This time it was a little more difficult. The car moved perhaps a little too slowly for the man ahead, so instead of accepting that I was complying with his order—a lone civilian in a sedan—he seemed to be getting

Weapons check at a Biafran ordnance base.

more agitated. I could see by the bars on his whites that he was a lieutenant commander. Waving his pistol wildly in the air, he shrieked, *"Come! Right now!"*

What next? I couldn't even make a run for it: the road was too narrow for me to quickly turn around. Anyway, by now he was just ahead of me. Perhaps twenty metres short of the gate—which I now saw was adorned with mounted machine guns—I pulled up. The naval officer was directly in front of me, shouting something incomprehensible and, to my surprise, was actually foaming at the mouth. Also, there was a crazed look in his eyes: he was smashed.

"What you want? What you want here?" he screamed, his voice rising an octave or two each time he called. I was terrified, though I dared not show it.

The rest of the troops, in varying levels of rage and stupefaction, surrounded the car. There were three or four rifles pointed at my head and more pressed into my body. In Nigeria's oppressive heat in those days you always drove with your windows open.

"Get out! Get out!" the lieutenant commander shouted. Anywhere else in the world the situation I had suddenly been thrust into would have been regarded as farcical, but just then this was pretty frightening. I actually believed that if I was not careful, I might be shot. The expatriate community in Lagos had already taken half a dozen casualties in the past twenty-four hours.

Many lives were lost in Nigeria in 1966 for no apparent reason. The great majority were Nigerian and not all were Ibo. It just happened and there was never anyone who would

Balair aid flight about to depart from Geneva for Biafra. (ICRC photo)

or could do anything about it. We, the public, only heard rumours, most times often exaggerated. The reason was simple: the moment the military took power they occupied the editorial offices of all the country's newspapers. Consequently, none of the events that should have been in the news were ever reported. Rumour, of course, feasted on its own excesses and that didn't help either.

"Lykes Lines ..." I called loudly. I had seen the offices of the American shipping line on an adjacent road as I approached the naval base and it seemed my only option. The officer stepped back a pace. He clearly hadn't a clue what I was talking about.

"Lykes Lines ... the American shipping line," I said once more, louder this time. The man was befuddled and it showed. My mentioning America must have made an impression and not necessarily a bad one because Washington had not looked kindly on the antics of General Aguiyi-Ironsi and his Ibo goons. The State Department had actually been quite vocal about the murders that had taken place six months earlier and the Nigerian press had reported most events surrounding the first coup because they were allowed to do so.

"What you mean? Lykes Lines! Lykes Lines! What you mean?" The man was shouting again.

I began to get out of the car because he had told me to do so earlier and I was simply complying with an order, but he moved quickly forward, pistol in my face and forced me back into the vehicle. "Stay there ... stay where you are! Do you hear?" There was no argument. It is not only in Africa that you don't argue with a man with a gun at your head.

Then, in a more direct approach, I mentioned the American shipping line once more and pointed toward the company's building across the way. The Nigerian officer turned and looked in that direction. By now all the soldiers around me were gesticulating wildly. Every one of them was shouting. One of them screamed, "Kill him! Kill the bastard! He knows he's not allowed here!"

Another man with a sub-machine gun—with the barrel close to my ear—demanded to know why I was spying? "Who you spy for?" he shouted. It was all so predictable and, let's face it, frighteningly intimidating.

Looking back, I realize today that none of it had the ingredients of a stage play or a film; it was simply too bizarre, it was also so damned repetitive. Since then, with the kind of work that I do, I have been involved in similar situations half a dozen times. Each time my skin crawls, as it does now writing about it. Each experience, I realize, seemed worse than the last: the frenzied rantings of soldiers often high on some substance or other and most times completely out of control. There never was any possibility of reasoning with such people. Once they had made up their minds that was it. Being white in a black man's country did not ease matters either. Also, I was on my own, and that hardly helped. Clearly, I was totally unprepared for what was happening to me on that lonely stretch of road in Apapa. I was aware, too, that if I did not keep my head, I could be killed, even by accident. By their actions some of these goons really did believe I was up to no good ... a mercenary perhaps. The papers were full of ghastly stories of mercenaries killing black people; events in the Congo were alive in the minds of these people.

Biafran anti-aircraft gun,
a latecomer to the war.

There was a solution of sorts, I suppose. It took a while, but I found that it was often better to counter this kind of hysteria with an offhand, friendly nonchalance. Any other approach, any belligerence, could lead to disaster. After I had mentioned the name Lykes Lines possibly twenty times—becoming quite vocal in my protestations, even though I smiled throughout—the officer eventually put his hands in the air to silence his men.

"Get back ... get back," he shouted at them. 'You!' he pointed at me. 'You get out of the car. Now!'

I did. I stood beside it with my hands in the air. Then, for the first time I saw that both machine guns on the turrets besides the main gate were trained directly on me. It had been that way probably throughout this terrifying pantomime, though if they were to shoot, they would probably have killed all of us in the road. I hoped that those manning it were sober—or at very least—no less drunk than the officer who was questioning me.

"Now, you say. What is your business?" he asked, his breath foul with booze.

I knew I had little time because his attention span was wavering. I explained in as few words as possible that Lykes Lines was an American shipping company. Its ships called regularly at Lagos. I pointed toward John Holt shipping documents which I had on my back seat in a pile. I had taken the more important papers from my office at Ikeja the day before, just in case. The officer looked carefully at me and then peered in through the rear window. What he saw seemed to placate him and then we went through the rigmarole again. It took at least fifteen or so more minutes of pretty convincing talk to get him to accept that I might not be someone with evil intent of overthrowing the Nigerian government and even then, he did so grudgingly. Obviously, my ready smile and nonchalance helped.

Eventually he allowed me to turn my car around. Once more, I did so slowly and very deliberately, all the while under the barrels of the guns on the turrets above the gates. As I drove those last few hundred metres along that lonely road, I could almost sense the aggression. God, I was glad to get away!

When I told them what had happened back at the club, some of the more experienced old coasters agreed that I had been extraordinarily lucky. Several Apapa residents had apparently been threatened by soldiers in the dock area earlier that day, I was told, one of them wounded by rifle fire, for no other reason, apparently, other than that he was there: the wrong place at the wrong time. Nigeria had transmogrified into armed chaos in less than two years.

Every one of us was more cautious after that. My steward, David, an Ibo, kept me informed of what was happening using his tribal grapevine as a conduit. Young Ibo males, he told me, were being pressured to return home and undergo military training, even though the Biafran war was still a year away. Quite a few he had befriended in Lagos, he said, had been shot.

3. NIGERIA SETS THE SCENE— BIAFRA LEADS THE WAY

Just how competent were the two armies facing each other? We have Frederick Forsyth saying that the Federal army could not fight its way out of a Human Rights convention in Blackpool. More to the point, they bolted if the enemy showed any defiance whatever. That these Nigerian troops made poor combatants was only part of it. They had their moments, of course, but the fact is that many of the regular officers running the show and making critical decisions—all the way to the top—were not much better. In fact, their job should have been simple because there were few full-blown campaigns while hostilities lasted, but rather, a series of minor or middle-range sorties and skirmishes.

For the Nigerian army that was just as well because whoever was handling things, like everyday planning, logistics, rations and movements, constantly seemed to make a hash of it. There were some operations that devolved into disasters even before they began. In 1967 alone—apart from the Biafran Mid-West invasion—these included early reversals at Eha Amufu, various abortive and disastrous Federal attempts to take Onitsha in an assault river-crossing, and the loss of previously captured ground like Oguede and Abalambie coconut estate. A year later, there were more catastrophes and, thereafter, more than a year of reversals befell Federal troops in numerous towns in the east.

British armoured cars being unloaded in Lagos prior to the start of hostilities (Author's photo)

We are not talking about a few months here, but the duration of the war: much of what happened on the various fronts devolved in a series of débâcles that had the Biafrans not been starved into submission they might possibly have won the war.

Nigerian army units would often be left to fend for themselves in total isolation, or more likely, troops would run out of ammunition, in large part because they had never been properly instructed in weapons-handling procedures. Rifles were thrust into the hands of green newcomers who were then rushed to the front and accidental discharges of firearms –ADs—were an everyday occurrence.

It eventually got so bad that on returning to barracks, soldiers were often forced to unload their weapons and leave their ammunition at the gates. They were resupplied before they again went into battle.

Take something as basic as fire and movement: such tactics hardly ever rated during the normal course of events on any of the front lines. In the overall course of the war it appeared that nobody had told the average Nigerian soldier that you did not raise your rifle above your head and pull the trigger on full automatic. More likely, they were put through the requisite paces but were simply not listening, or very possibly, were drunk when they went into battle.

Worse, those doing the fighting had no experience of the kind of jungle terrain into which they were thrust. Most were city or town boys with good dollops of jail birds who were about as interested in going to war as they might have been in solving equations. To most of them the jungle was as alien as swimming in the sea. Suicides happened a lot, especially among the better educated.

As for basics like drill, square-bashing, it simply was not on the cards, which also meant that unit parades—if they happened at all—would be shambolic.

One insight came from Biafra where Major Jan Breytenbach's small force was training rebel troops intended for a Special Forces role. A new intake arrived and during a small-arms

Nigerian frigate at Apapa docks, Lagos. (Author's photo)

training session, one of the recruits was seen firing his weapon into the air. When asked what he thought he was doing, he replied that because his rifle was an automatic, "the bullets are able find the target on their own". Those of us who covered other African conflicts are aware that these things happen, sometimes more often than most instructors would like. I have even observed Sudanese fighters close their eyes when they let rip with the heavy stuff.

For all that, the capabilities of the Nigerian army could sometimes be as changeable as the West African weather. They would start quite well, take ground, overrun towns, defeat rebel strong points and then, a month or three later, would end up losing much of it.

It was sheer force of numbers that ultimately made them victorious, by which time they outnumbered their Biafrans by something like ten to one, though there are some who maintained that the margin was significantly greater toward the end. Also, the Nigerian army was issued with rations on a reasonably regular basis, while Ojukwu's troops had almost no food at all, a situation which customarily favours the aggressor.

Case in point here was after having gained much ground in early 1968, the Biafran army hit back hard and overran the Federal army at several points. Six months later, in October 1968, Colonel Benjamin Adekunle's so-called crack commandos lost a third of their number when this force took a serious thumping by the Biafran army at Umuahia. Taking back Owerri from the Nigerians is today regarded in eastern Nigeria as one of the touchstone actions of the war and clearly, the fact that Ojukwu had the support of locals, this situation certainly played a vital role in his overall strategy.

New recruits in the Biafran army (Author's photo)

In spite of all that, the Nigerians eventually won their war, though it took an army of 150,000 men backed by an incredibly efficient mercenary-led air force to achieve this, even though the average Biafran soldier toward the end was so weak and malnourished it took two of them to lift an ammunition case.

According to Colonel Robert E. Scott, defence attaché at the British high commission in Lagos at the time, it was a consistently sub-par performance by the Nigerian army and something that every military representative in Lagos could hardly miss. The colonel went on to write a critical report on the capabilities of the Nigerian army (or lack thereof) for his superiors in London toward the end of the war. Though classified, it was subsequently leaked to the *Daily Telegraph*.

By now, Ojukwu had secretly launched a fairly extensive build-up of arms involving people like Hank Wharton and Rhodesia's Jack Malloch, a flamboyant and extremely competent aviator who ended up smuggling weapons all over Africa. Both Wharton and Malloch—together with arms merchants from France, Holland, Germany and China—worked hand-in-glove with several European governments including France, Portugal and Spain to give Ojukwu just about all that he needed.

By linking itself to Paris's subterfuge, South Africa also got involved. The plan orchestrated by Jacques Foccart, the Elysée's shadowy *eminence grise* in charge of African affairs

A Biafran hospital hit by Nigerian MiG fighters (ICRC photo)

A Biafran cannon on an improvised mounting.

for President de Gaulle, was to try to help Pretoria out of the isolation that had resulted from its years of race-motivated policies. Soon after hostilities in the Congo ended, France persuaded South Africa to provide the secessionists with arms and ammunition, largely because French ammunition did not fit 'British standard' Biafran weapons.

Pretoria eventually provided Ojukwu with hundreds of tons of ordnance as well as a handful of Special Forces troops, though, as Forsyth comments, they were kept extremely low profile. In the end there were mercenaries from a variety of nations in Biafra, but it was always tough going: factors included the isolation of the rebel state, erratic or non-existent communications, shortages of food and munitions, all coupled to a harsh tropical climate in a region that for decades had been dubbed 'the armpit of Africa' was only part of it. The Biafrans were good fighters but they lacked the kind of practical 'on the ground' tactical advice that these old war dogs could give. Also they would not always follow the advice of others, which meant that the mercenary presence, limited to start with, ultimately had little impact on the outcome of the war.

Mercenary cadres would also be faced with an entrenched level of bias from the Biafran officer corps. Most of these black soldiers believed that they could do a damn side better than a nondescript bunch of 'hired guns' and they weren't shy to say so.

Among the foreigners involved, not everybody turned a coin. Count Gustav von Rosen, a Swedish nobleman of independent means created an instant air force for the near-planeless Biafrans during one of his summer vacations and he did not charge a penny. When he flew his squadron of second-hand MFI-9B Swedish MiniCons into Biafra from Gabon, they were so heavily loaded with extra fuel tanks, rockets in wing-pods and radio equipment, that some of the

Count Carl Gustaf von Rosen who donated the MiniCons to Biafra.

aviators present at takeoff at Libreville airport said they would not get off the ground. Well they did, and within the first couple of days these tiny aircraft, originally built as trainers, had notched up their first successful strikes. In the first three raids after arriving in the rebel territory, the MiniCons struck at airports at Benin City and Port Harcourt and bagged several Nigerian air force aircraft—including a MiG-17 or two as well as an Egyptian air force Ilyushin-28—all blasted while still on the ground. By then the Nigerians had started using Egyptian mercenaries to fly some of the larger jets that included Ilyushin bombers. After that, the Biafran pilots had to be more circumspect: there were any number of Nigerian air force planes—including MiGs—out searching for them and their bases.

Ilyushin tactical bomber of the Nigerian air force.

43

Biafran troops marching. (Author's photo)

Another figure from Africa's dubious past that arrived in the war was Rolf Steiner, the same man who was later captured by the Sudanese government while fighting for the Christian rebels in the south. Before that, in Biafra, Steiner was appointed brigade commander; there were mercenaries from many nations who eventually fought under him. An austere, engaging figure, he'd enlisted in the French Foreign Legion after Germany's surrender in 1945 and claimed to have spent seven years in Indochina, where he lost a lung at Dien Bien Phu, which Forsyth, in doing a bit of detective work of his own, said wasn't true. That did not prevent Steiner scrapping for another five years in Algeria, after which he broke away and joined the anti-Gaullist OAS. While living in Paris, he got wind of opportunities in West Africa and it took him only a few months to make colonel in Ojukwu's army, a commendable touch since he'd never been more than a sergeant before.

For all his faults, which included insubordination toward his Biafran seniors, Steiner was extremely tough on his troops. Black or white, they found him a ruthless taskmaster. But somehow, they seemed to respect him because while he was unconventional in his approach to most things, he got results. The proponent of the unexpected till the last, his favourite ploy was to haul out his Browning Hi-Power pistol and fire it into the air whenever he demanded attention. In Africa, such quirks work. For his personal credo he adopted the Legion's motto: 'Long live death, long live war'.

Early in the war, Steiner was involved in an aborted attempt to form a Biafran navy. With Biafra ringed by conflict on three sides—and the great Niger river and its tributaries running through most of it—it was to be expected that Ojukwu would do what he could to ease the Nigerian naval blockade. Federal forces by then included a Dutch frigate, five Ford-class seaward defence boats (SDBs) and three Soviet P6-class patrol boats. At one stage, a Biafran contingent tried to seize one of the SDBs in Port Harcourt harbour but those involved were thwarted by the quick action of a Nigerian support group who sank the boat at its moorings. In a bid to outdo them, Steiner and Georgio Norbiato, a former Italian marine commando who had previously fought in the Congo, commandeered three fast Chris-Craft (luxury powerboats) from the Port Harcourt sailing club. They mounted machine guns on the prows and set to work. Each could carry four commandos plus a pilot, the idea being that they would ambush small freighters moving upriver.

Their first sortie provided excellent dividends, the booty including five Land Rovers, thousands of uniforms and millions of 7.62mm cartridges. A later haul brought in ten tons of Soviet mortar shells and a good supply of grenades as well as several 20mm Oerlikon cannons that had been mounted specifically to thwart such actions.

Then everything ground to a halt after Norbiato was killed in a contact. Until the end of the war, mercernary elements continued to use the Niger Delta to perform early-warning patrols.

First Big Strike

Biafra's military forces started well to begin with, because basically many of their officers were seasoned professionals, some having trained at British military establishments from where they quite often went on to do duty with United Nations forces in the Congo and elsewhere.

Bayonet training in the rebel territory. (Author's photo)

In-flight photo of a NAF Delphin.

Biafran refugees fleeing the conflict.

Frederick Forsyth was in Biafra when Lieutenant-Colonel Ojukwu decided to invade Nigeria westwards, toward Lagos. It was a bold step, this former BBC correspondent recalls, though he broke with that news organization soon afterwards because of its biased reports about the war.

Explained Forsyth, "Yes, I went in with them. We swept across the Onitsha Bridge and very soon we could see that it was a crazy amateurish kind of war, a conflict, in a sense, of boy scouts. Here was this huge bridge spanning the great Niger river that effectively connected the Biafran Eastern Region with Western Nigeria. There was a sort of gentleman's agreement in place between the leaders of both sides not to use it. They had another agreement not to destroy it. Certainly, it was accepted by all that it would not be used for any kind of invasion. Ojukwu was regarded by the Nigerian military leader Colonel Yakubu Gowon as an absolute bastard for breaking that concord by crossing the bridge with an invasion force. In a way it was a bit like the mouse that roared. How, Gowon asked, thoroughly perplexed, could the tiny little Eastern Region invade Nigeria? But it did. And it was a remarkably successful venture because the newly appointed Nigerian leader's strategy was a disaster.

"Gowon, by now at the head of the rest of Nigeria, took the entire professional Nigerian Army of only 6,000 men and hurled them across the Benue river [a tributary of the Niger] to the north of the rebel enclave. He then ordered them to turn their guns toward the south and face Biafra, where they promptly bogged down. The result was that there were barely any troops between the bridge across the Niger river at Onitsha and Lagos, Nigeria's capital* The Biafran strike force was faced with an absolutely empty, open road to victory.

"Someone got to Ojukwu and said to him, look we can be in Lagos in forty-eight hours of hard motoring. That would end the war at a stroke. I don't know how much persuading he took, but certainly, that was what he finally decided to do.

"Since Ojukwu had no armoured columns of his own, the Biafrans got together a bunch of trucks, mammy wagons and oil tankers because they would need fuel supplies. They also grabbed just about every Land Rover in the country and commandeered oil company vehicles and virtually the entire region's agricultural four-by-fours. And what a motley collection that lot soon became, though all these shortcomings did not prevent the force from calling itself 'Ojukwu's Undefeated'.

"They hadn't enough soldiers in their territory, because broadly speaking, Ojukwu apart, the Ibos had never really been among the country's soldier class. Nigeria's army in fact—its outstanding cadre of officers apart—was overwhelmingly from the North, much as it is today. So what this fighting colonel got in lieu of a combat force was a bunch of rag-tag, bobtail volunteers, many of them schoolboys.

"So too with his officer corps, which was mainly composed of technical officers. The head of the Biafran Army, for instance, was a former Nigerian Signals Corps man.

---

* It was only after the war ended that Lagos ceased being the Nigerian capital. Abuja, a large town—and now a major city—near the centre of the country was chosen for that role.

Above and below: A Nigerian convoy hit by Biafran troops.

He was very good with radios, but sadly, he didn't know a damn thing about guns, though they had some artillery officers because that was a technical discipline. But there was no armour at all. They were literally riding to war in trucks, lorries, tankers, and Land Rovers.

"So this column, before dawn one morning—as I was to see for myself because I was with them—drove across that crucial bridge and took the war to the rest of the nation. Without formality, they swept aside the two dozen or so Nigerian soldiers on the western side and plunged on toward Lagos. They reached Benin City, the capital of the Mid-West within twelve hours where, amazingly, they lost their nerve. They just could not believe that they had managed to penetrate so deep into Nigeria without encountering any kind of opposition.

"Yet even then they did not stop. This improvised, totally makeshift force—still with me in tow—went beyond Benin, actually to the border between the Mid-West state and Western Nigeria, which is a little village called Ore. It was there that some of us realized that the reality of reaching the capital, Lagos, was almost in sight.

"Then too, the word 'cut off' began to circulate. 'Cut off from what?' I asked several of them. 'What are you going to be cut off from, in your own country?'

"'We're cut off,' they answered, adding that there might be Nigerian troops suddenly appearing behind us.

"So I would question where these supposed Nigerian troops were supposed to be coming from? There really aren't any there, I told the commander and his staff, 'Oh,' they answered, 'still, we might be cut off.' Very soon, the expression 'cut off' became obsessional.

"At the start of the invasion, Colonel Ojukwu did something rather unusual by appointing one of the very few Yorubas in his army, Brigadier Victor Banjo, as the commanding officer of the entire expedition. He thought that because Banjo was a Yoruba, he would be made welcome once he entered his own Yorubaland. What the Biafran leader did not recognize was that Banjo had his own agenda. The original intention of this rather enterprising but devious Yoruba officer—with all this power play then going on—was that he earnestly intended becoming the future ruler of Nigeria.

"So Banjo turned traitor. Once the column stopped in Benin City, he used the radio of the British Deputy High

Rockets fired by Nigerian forces displayed by a Biafran soldier. (Author's photo)

Biafran troops practise fire and movement. (Author's photo)

Commissioner in Benin City to call up the British High Commission in Lagos and ask for Gowon to be brought to the microphone. His intention was to negotiate a handover of the country to himself. Banjo wanted to call himself President of Nigeria.

"That bit of duplicity stopped the invasion in its tracks, though frankly, I could never understand why. I could never comprehend why this extremely successful invasion force—with a completely empty road ahead—had been halted.

"Of course, there were two reasons here. The one was a total loss of nerve, and of course the treachery by Brigadier Banjo, its commanding officer."

Ojukwu himself admitted afterwards that the role played by Victor Banjo—a non-Ibo, but one of his senior planners—had a significant effect on the outcome of that early, extremely critical phase. His forces were never supposed to have taken the Mid-West city of Benin. They wasted weeks and a lot of lives in doing so. Then Banjo clandestinely made contact with Federal officers in Lagos. It did not work, because Banjo was unmasked, court-martialled and shot at dawn.

Throughout it all, the experience—as that experienced British author will tell you— taught Nigeria a very hard lesson. It set in motion the effort, as he states, to recruit, recruit and recruit. Forsyth again: "Within almost no time at all, Gowon ran his army up from the original 6,000 to something like 150,000 ... The newcomers in the Nigerian Army came from all over. They scraped dregs out of the prisons, like Lagos's awful Kirikiri Prison,

The first of the mercenaries arrive in Nigeria (Ares Klootwyk collection)

which was nearly emptied of every thug, gangster and killer. Murderers were summarily released and put into uniform.

"Then they virtually emptied Lagos University. They put the students in uniform, gave them rifles, and, as was the case in Angola thirty years later, all these men were pushed up to the front. There was never any question of training this new group of improvised soldiers.

"Suddenly, further afield, there were other effects. There were people in London and Washington who panicked when they realized that perhaps this Nigerian civil war thing was not going to be as easy as they'd originally thought."

4. WAR GATHERS PACE IN THE EAST

After Lieutenant-Colonel Ojukwu's aborted attempt to hit Lagos, hostilities entered a new and more determined phase. British and Soviet military aid became more pronounced and the Biafrans had to start organizing a mammoth series of relief flights from 'friendly' airports, if only to keep its people from starvation.

And starvation it was, as I discovered on my very first morning in the rebel enclave. Nobody had warned me that I should take my own food, lots of it. So when I eventually touched down on Uli's primitive jungle airstrip—it was surrounded by the wrecks of aircraft that had not made it, either on landing or takeoff—I expected to find the rudiments of a wartime canteen. There was nothing. Even the two slices of bread I received an hour or two after checking in was half sawdust. I was given a cup of tea and it had the flavour of what I'd imagine to be a banana leaf.

It was hard to grasp at first that Biafra was completely surrounded by the enemy. At best, 200 tons of ammunition was being brought in each night that the airstrip remained open. Whenever Uli was knocked out—it happened fairly often—there would be nothing coming in for days. That was serious, especially since Ojukwu's army needed to keep 100,000 or more Federal Nigerians at bay.

Also, throughout hostilities, the casualty rate rose steadily. It puzzled us all, considering that this was a strictly African war, how the Biafrans were able to hold out so long? There were several reasons.

A Christian wedding in Calabar.

The nightly flights into Biafra, which concentrated mainly on the needs of the children and the military, could hardly have been expected to supply the demands of several million people cut off from the world outside. As a result, prices in Biafra were the highest in Africa.

A 'meal' of roots at the Progress Hotel in Owerri for example, cost the equivalent of two dollars, an ounce of meat as much again. Salt for the meal would be priced at one Biafran pound or two U.S. dollars, all of which we had to exchange on our arrival with our foreign currencies, at par with sterling at pre-secession rates. By the end of the war, inflation was rising at several hundred percent a month.

The cost of non-essential goods was even greater. A single cigarette in the last two months of the conflict cost ten Biafran shillings or roughly a dollar. So did a 'real' cup of tea with goat's milk (I was surprised that any goats had survived so long). What sugar was available mostly went to mission hospitals where it was used as a substitute for glucose intended for starving children.

Petrol (as they still called it) was a strategic material and not sold on the open market, although a gallon could be bought easily enough on the black market for $30 or $40, and then only in American dollars. A pair of men's flannels cost $20, a shirt sometimes as much as $50. Second-hand clothes were barely any cheaper and it puts things in perspective when you realize that half a century ago, that was a lot of money.

I was soon confronted by inflation. After breakfast on my first morning at State House, I was told to wait because there was no transport, something I soon got used to. The morning newspaper arrived: a single folded sheet of school exercise paper that, I was assured, had a circulation that ran well into four figures. I was charged a dollar.

"It's the only paper we've left," said the youthful editor of *Jet,* the Biafran daily; "but it gives us what we need: objective news of the outside world." Anything from Federal Nigeria was tainted propaganda.

The news was printed in bright red ink, which looked like a compound of shoe polish and ochre and probably was, because the Biafrans certainly did not have the cash to spare for the real thing. That particular issue of 4 November 1969 celebrated Ojukwu's thirty-sixth birthday. Half-page advertisements on the crammed sheet had been taken by two expatriate companies that had formerly traded in the Eastern Region: the United Africa Company (Unilever) and the African Continental Bank, last heard with its head office in Lagos. A two-column advertisement on the last page of *Jet* urged subscribers to book in time for their Christmas cards and New Year greetings.

All foreign companies that formerly operated in eastern Nigeria were managed by their Ibo staff and though little happened—for instance at the local office of Caterpillar, or Bata shoes—many were surprised after the war ended to find that nearly every branch office had kept their books completely up to date.

In spite of some lighter moments, the grim reality of conflict was omnipresent. Cripples were everywhere and there were a lot of them. Young boys, some barely into their teens, hobbled legless on crutches. Anywhere else they'd have been in an institution, or being prepared for prosthetics. Only the very worst cases could be dealt with at Red Cross and

A Nigerian mammy wagon, the kind the Biafrans used to move their wounded back from the front lines.

government clinics. I came across several groups of shell-shocked youngsters— these were experiences that remained fixed in my mind—and huddled in small groups almost like zombies, they communicated with grunts and gestures in an absent-minded sort of way. Most were tended by some older person until they recovered. Quite a few got better and some were even posted back to their units. Quite a number, one of the Red Cross people told me, never would. Decades later, some of these poor souls are still afflicted.

Biafra's ability to survive, it was agreed afterwards by those of us who were able to observe conditions from up close, was due largely to the remarkable competence of the ordinary Biafran.

This was—and still is—a community that is able to improvise, plan for the unexpected and take the initiative. As we have already seen, their adversaries, often disparagingly, call eastern Nigerians the Jews of Africa and of course they're right. Ibos like to roll up their sleeves and get things done.

Also, easterners like to make money; they work and succeed where others fail. Like the Luo in Kenya and the Mandingo of Guinea, they are sometimes thoroughly disliked by less pushy tribes, much like southerners are wary of New Yorkers in the US. It's a patchy analogy, but you get the picture. In that regard (with notable exceptions) they are consequently very different when compared to the average Yoruba, Hausa or Fulani. Success, as they often say, breeds distrust.

What I did discover with time, because I had become friendly with many Ibos, is that I'd put my life in their hands any day of the week, which is not something us foreigners are likely to do too often on the African continent. We, who favoured the Ibos, also shared somewhat in their unpopularity. Frederick Forsyth resigned his job at the BBC not because he was vociferously committed to the Biafran cause, but because the British Broadcasting Corporation ended up being partisan in a conflict where, in keeping with a tradition that went back to its first days on air, should have shown impartiality. It was all oil politics, we knew, and in the end it made a difference.

Richard Hall, one of the most experienced Africa hands, was greatly taken by this rebel community. Dick, as we all knew him, was the cofounder and editor of Zambia's *Central Africa Mail* and no newcomer to this volatile continent. His comments about Biafra are instructive. Hall described Biafrans in the *Sunday Times* of London at the time as "a people I respect and like [who] are threatened with persecution and death. I cannot therefore pretend to be impartial. But Biafra is more than a human tragedy: it is the first place I've been to in Africa where the Africans themselves are truly in charge ... where there is a sense of nationhood ... free from the African vices of graft, superstition and ignorance."

It had all suddenly become an extraordinarily furious debate.

Some of the best stories to come out of Biafra were not so much about the ongoing conflict, as the ability of the Biafrans to do their own thing and, certainly, they were ingenious. We could walk through any Biafran town, even toward the end of the war and discover that life went on almost as if nothing were happening. Shops were open, though their stock was exiguous, post offices were selling stamps and money orders and, with fair warning, you could even buy foreign exchange in the banks, although you had to have good reason. There were dozens of home industries repairing or recycling old things or making new ones: iron bedsteads, car engines rebored on makeshift lathes, stoves rebuilt, and of course, the market mammies at their stalls. The army took most of what was left after a proportion had been set aside for the children, so their offerings were skimpy.

French medics near the front: the Biafran embryo of Médecins Sans Frontières. (Author's photo)

All that was what you were actually *allowed* to see: obviously, there was much else besides. Behind the towns, in forest and bush clearings, hundreds of factories turned out all sorts of things, such as boots for soldiers and ammunition. Emeka, a soldier who was detached from his unit, guided me through some of them. In a factory near Umuahia, engineers were making—or rather recycling—motor parts for an otherwise ageing fleet of army trucks, mostly mammy-wagons that had been seized. Brake-linings, I was told, were among many items on the so-called 'Urgent List', which was one of the reasons why some were modified from crashed aircraft parts at Uli.

There were more jungle workshops making uniforms. Since there was no cloth, long lines of women were busy manufacturing on primitive factory tables a rough substitute from bark. It was not the best or most supple material and was probably tough on the skin but it was better than nothing. The same held with army boots, which the military needed in volume, though an astonishing number of Biafran soldiers wore footwear that once belonged to Nigerian soldiers who would not be needing them again. Since there was no leather, they added chemicals to a raw rubber latex mixture and created a strong and pliable material for the uppers. The soles were made from old motor-vehicle tyres.

They refined their own oil in cooking-pot refineries, rather like illicit Arkansas liquor stills. Right up to the end Biafran improvisers produced enough fuel to keep several hundred vehicles running.

A children's refugee camp in Biafra. (Author's photo)

The *Times* in London ran a fairly comprehensive report on 5 March 1969 on Biafra's ongoing local oil supplies. It explained that apart from military needs, church groups, the Red Cross (ICRC) as well as other aid groups, all received weekly allocations of diesel fuel which totalled about 1,000 gallons. This was significant, it declared because Biafra had been under a naval and land blockage since the previous July. At a Biafran army divisional headquarters I saw one of their homemade refineries in action. The man in charge, an economics graduate of Durham university, Mr Nwofili Adibuah, aged thirty-four explained: "The process we use is fractional distillation using these crude cooking pots ... The petrol comes off first, then the kerosene and finally the diesel," adding that his particular mini-refinery consisted of three "cooking pots and produced 280 gallons of petroleum, 100 gallons of kerosene and 250 gallons of diesel every day."

There were even private citizens refining their own fuel in their eastern Nigerian backyards to keep their cars on the road. Dr Ben Nwosu, a distinguished Biafran nuclear physicist, who trained in London and the United States and worked at the International Atomic Energy Agency in Vienna, told me that his main refinery, which was considerably more sophisticated than what I had been shown, produced 25,000 gallons of fuel each day "and we are now investigating the possibility of making our own aviation fuel ... But we do more than produce equipment for the army. We have decided to produce what we call survival gin, which has palm wine at its base. Until we lost Abakaliki we were able to produce our own salt. Also, we manufacture our own matches, dyes for military clothing, soap made from palm oil as well as caustic soda, shoe polish and farm implements."

It was the little everyday things about life in a country at war that astonished those of us who visited Biafra for the first time. We discovered an inordinate will to survive, which was natural enough, except that the odds were powerfully stacked against Ojukwu's people. I saw conditions at fairly close quarters since my escort Emeka and I went just about everywhere on foot. Cars or pick-ups were a luxury reserved for longer trips.

The Biafran social code was enforced with the rigour of an Amish settlement in Pennsylvania and criminal courts were held from Monday to Friday in all big towns in the rebel enclave. The Biafran supreme court of appeal sat in session in Owerri when it was in rebel hands or in Umuahia when it wasn't. Colonial traditions were strictly observed: wigs and robes for all senior members of the bar, which was absurd in that climate, except that such flummeries still persist in most of the former British territories, except that wigs are no longer worn in British courts. Nor had the prisons been abolished. Inmates could be seen in working parties under guard on the last day of the war.

Ojukwu printed his own money, now of good value among collectors. The notes, gaudy and in every colour of the spectrum, were professionally printed in Europe. A planeload of it disappeared on the way back from Switzerland. Biafra also had its own coins, stamps and postal orders. In spite of restrictions necessitated by conflict and a breakdown in communications, Biafran welfare officers continued to pay pensions to war widows until the end and postal deliveries always remained efficient, even after hostilities ended.

When an area had to be evacuated—as in the case of Owerri before its recapture (following the fall of Umuahia to the east)—the first to be moved were the wounded and civil prisoners,

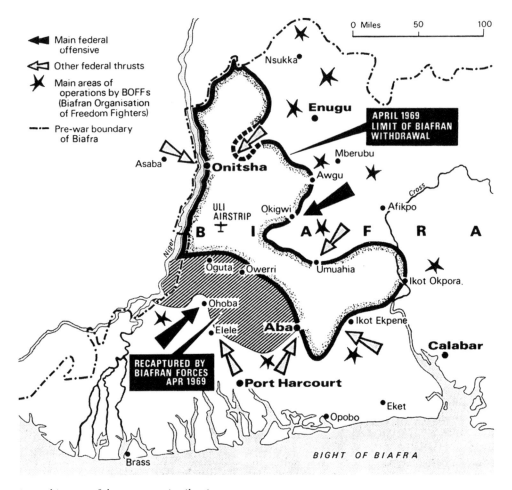

A graphic map of the war as at April 1969.

the latter carrying litters or supplies. Likewise, entire hospitals disappeared into the bush. Former inmates of mental institutions had long since been released to fend for themselves in the jungle and from what I heard, they seemed to manage. Federal troops never touched them because African tribal lore disavows anybody doing so: it is very bad juju to abuse the insane.

For much of the war, Uli—through which I was channelled in and out of the country—remained the tenuous lifeline between Biafra and the world outside. The 'miracle of Uli' as those who saw it first-hand called it, hosted these precarious flights that were often loaded well beyond safety limits. Hundreds of aircraft ran the Federal blockade each week, but not always without incident because quite a few were destroyed either on the ground or in landing or takeoff accidents. Many more suffered shrapnel damage. Some were hit while taxiing, others were bombed by the Nigerian air force 'Intruder', an antiquated C-47 Dakota that had been adapted to carry 20-kilogram canisters of explosives. Later, the Nigerians bought some surplus American World War II bombers.

There were several planes also accidentally shot down by Biafran ground fire, though the rebels always denied it: they said it couldn't happen. But it did. We were nearly hit by heavy machine-gun fire from the ground as we came in, and it wasn't Nigerian fire coming up at us because their lines were miles away.

Look at the figures. In church relief flights alone (never mind the arms runs which were a sizeable tally each night) there were 7,350 freight flights into Biafra in the three years that war ravaged eastern Nigeria. In this time almost a million tons of supplies, including arms, were taken into the beleaguered territory. During the course of these operations there were 15 aircraft lost and 25 aircrew killed, all buried at a small cemetery adjacent to Uli airport. Their graves were bulldozed by the Nigerian army immediately after the war ended. That took place a day or two after Nigerian troops had overrun Uli, so that, as one cocky Nigerian field commander declared to a gathering of foreign correspondents, "they'll be eternally forgotten ... we don't want their families poking about here for their remains afterwards."

The actual landing process was dicey. With time, routines to cope with the unusual demands of the bush strip were developed, with the result that our descent was ultra-steep. Pilots would manoeuvre their aircraft into position before sets of improvised runway lights were switched on for about five or six seconds. That was all the time they had to get their bearings. Meanwhile, our pilot Herman was talking to ground control, or rather, I hoped that he was doing so. Though the world was dark outside, most of the pilots would have some idea of where they were while circling because of the landing lights that flashed irregularly before touchdown. Once into short finals, another few seconds of light was allowed and that was that. It was pretty precise operation and spoke a lot for the skill of those at the controls of these ageing hulks: many of the pilots were retired airline veterans and were well past their 'use-by' dates.

It was the job of a Nigerian air force bomber labelled 'Genocide' by locals—also flown by mercenaries—to give these relief planes a battering. The 'bomber' would break into the cargo planes' radio chatter and taunt them: "This is Genocide, baby ... come on down and get killed."

The man's South African accent was unmistakeable: obviously another war dog. As Forsyth still recalls, "anyone listening in on the same wavelength could hear mercenary pilots flying the Nigerian bombers jeering at them, daring them to land when the lights flashed those few elusive seconds."

To begin with 'Genocide' was an antiquated Dakota C-47 'Gooney Bird' that had been adapted to carry canisters of explosives. Later the Nigerians would acquire surplus American B-25s. The 'interventionist' aircraft would hover at about 18,000 feet and wait for things to happen, the idea being to drop his canisters just as an incoming aircraft came into the approach. Ideally, the explosives would detonate just as the plane had its wheels on the strip. This improvised bomber, and another dubbed 'Intruder', rarely succeeded in causing serious damage. But when they did, the Nigerian propaganda machine would spin into action and Lagos newspapers would crow that Uli airport had been crippled.

Biafran refugees fleeing Federal MiGs (ICRC photo)

It sometimes took a week to put things right again and often Ojukwu's people would find alternate stretches of road. Then the process would begin all over again.

A sidebar to these events was that in their final approach to Uli airport, many pilots would come in so low that their fuselage would sometimes clip the tops of palms. Later, back at base, aircrews would compare notes about 'green props'. Just about everybody experienced them.

There was also the occasional 'red prop'. Since most loading teams were made up of tribesmen who knew little about the dangers of modern aircraft, there were instances of them walking into propellers while the planes were being cleared.

Once on the ground, Biafrans crews—so many of them clearly malnourished—went to work, sometimes with astonishing gusto considering that they were starving. Obviously with the 'bomber' overhead, and none of the pilots wishing to spend more immobile time on the ground than was absolutely necessary, there was a very real urgency to it all. Aircrews would keep their engines ticking over and cargoes would be cleared within ten to fifteen minutes.

If it were food, Roman Catholic White Fathers in their long cassocks would direct operations. Munitions were handled by the Biafran army and canisters and crates destined for the military would be hurried away in trucks. Meanwhile other Biafran officials would indicate what or who was to go out that night. Most of the outgoing cargoes consisted of starving, mostly orphaned children who were sent off to camps in other parts of Africa such as Kilometre Onze in Gabon or to a succession of Catholic institutions in São Tomé.

The Biafrans were taking out a thousand tons of cacao and copra a month on these planes.

None of us who went into Biafra on those illegal flights at night will ever forget the heat and the noise that cloaked us like a sauna once we stepped off the plane. I crouched in a split-pole bunker beside the runway, together with a couple of others, with a musty, unwashed immediacy to it all. Intermittently the senses were sharpened by the stutter of automatic fire along the runway somewhere.

Alongside our position were several tall palms, their foliage blown away. This was all that was left of what was once a substantial palm oil plantation that dated from the colonial era. Their trunks looked like thousands of giant, naked fingers pointing toward the sky. Alongside, perhaps thirty paces away, was the barely recognizable tail section of a Joint Church Aid Globemaster C-97 that had crashed a month before.

That, the priests in their robes, occasional bursts of automatic fire, coupled to the roar of engines of aircraft landing and taking off made for something surreal. Herman, our pilot did not even bother to wave goodbye. He was airborne again in minutes. For a while an uneasy calm descended on the jungle, broken only occasionally by more automatic fire.

An Ibo officer—a captain, I think, with the distinctive Biafran rising sun patch on his arm came toward me at a brisk pace. He cradled a Sten gun. "I take it that you are Mister

Painting a giant red cross on the runway at Uli. (ICRC photo)

Venter of the *Daily Express*?" he asked with a salute and an accent more reminiscent of Guildford than Africa. It was all so terribly British.

As with Iraq, almost forty years later, Nigeria's oil almost overnight became a priority. As we have seen, it lay at the hub of Nigeria's problems. Huge deposits of fossil fuels had been discovered earlier along the coast of the Eastern Region and Nigeria was changed forever. Looking back, West Africa's 'black gold' seems always to have been a curse. Even today there is much squabbling about who owns what, whether title to concessions are legal or even whether existing oil claims that have been tapped for decades are even valid or obtained 'by other means'. More recently, Nigeria and the Cameroon Republic almost went to war over who owns an obscure stretch of land called the Bakassi Peninsula, a place very few of us had ever heard of before. In fact, nobody knew it even existed until oil was discovered there. The Cameroons eventually acquiesced and Bakassi is today Nigerian. There was more sabre-rattling over what exactly constituted the offshore rights of Equatorial Guinea, formerly Spanish Guinea. A botched mercenary attempt to oust the president of that island government, one of the most brutal and corrupt countries on the globe followed. It was led by among others, Mark Thatcher, son of former British prime minister Margaret Thatcher, and Simon Mann, ex-SAS scion of a prominent English brewing family.

Looking back at some of the events that took place in the mid-1960s, it is clear that the Ibos were way ahead of their Nigerian compatriots at being able to appreciate the bigger picture. Effectively, they did not want the 'Backward North' to enjoy any of it: the commodity was rightfully theirs, was it not? It was about then that developed nations—Britain, America, France and Russia in particular—began to look seriously at the military implications involved. It was quite obvious to anybody who travelled about the country that Nigeria was headed for trouble, though at that stage, the prospect of a civil war was remote. Nonetheless, it was a complicated issue because internecine strife—as we have since seen in Chechnya, Kashmir, Sri Lanka, Iraq, Afghanistan, Lebanon and elsewhere – always is.

5. GOWON AND OJUKWU

As Frederick Forsyth, one of Colonel Ojukwu's trusted friends, confirmed after the killing had been briefly halted, "beyond the frontiers of the soon-to-be rebel state, Ibos were given an incredibly hard time, especially since the entire defence structure had been 'ethnically cleansed': Easterners who had survived the initial violent purge were given their marching orders."

The appointment of a new head of state, a rather youthful regular lieutenant-colonel by the name of Yakubu Gowon, or 'Jack' as we got to know him, was a welcome development. He was clearly British-trained and as far as we knew, did not drink or smoke dope, which was an enormous plus because so many of his colleagues did. I would spot him coming to Ikeja airport from time to time, but these were quiet, unobtrusive visits that were obviously low key: they lacked the fanfare of his predecessors. His security detail was most times kept to a minimum and, from what I gathered, his drive to Ikeja after things had settled down, was usually a two-car affair. Other times he would be preceded by motorcycle outriders and sirens: then we all had to stop and give way.

At that early stage, there was very little known about the man who was more of the 'power behind the throne' than somebody who had seized the initiative in Nigeria's second military takeover. In fact, he had a minor role in the July 1966 counter-coup and emerged as a compromise head of the new government for several reasons. First, he was regarded by most to be 'neutral'. More salient, he was never perceived—either by friend or foe—as being power hungry. It was a sensible choice of leader.

General Yakubu Gowon, as he became, was a mild-mannered soldier who came from a small northern tribe, the Angas. Forsyth told me when we discussed the man that he remembers him emerging out of the escalating chaos as a mild-mannered adjutant of the Nigerian army: "He was the typical young Nigerian officer ... More important, he wasn't a Muslim. In fact, he was a devout Christian and being, as it was termed 'Middle Belt'—neither from the north nor the south, he couldn't be tarred with a brush of being an Ibo." In fact, Forsyth reckons, he suited just about everybody.

As far as the coup leaders were concerned, their attitude was that they could run the country behind this man. So too with Sir David Hunt, the British high commissioner: he was the perfect choice. "Sir David was very much old colonial school. He liked the fact that Gowon would snap to attention whenever he walked in ... that pleased the man no end. In contrast, there were those among us who regarded the Nigerian military leader as an overgrown boy scout," Forsyth commented.

A career army officer, Gowon was regarded a cut above the rest and though a contemporary of the rebel leader Ojukwu, they shared little else, before or after the mutiny. The two men had actually served in the same units on occasion and knew and understood

General Yakubu
Gowon.

each other's foibles, which could have been one of the reasons the Biafran leader believed that he could pull off his gamble.

Whereas the future rebel leader wasn't afraid to go before the microphone to put his views across, Gowon wasn't one for publicity. In fact, it took us an age to get our first interview with a man whom I always found extremely reserved and quiet-spoken. Never recalcitrant, he was reticent to talk about his own life and though he could have claimed one of the presidential palaces as his own, he never did. All his successors did, most times with excessive brass and hoopla. He, in turn, preferred to stay on in the barracks with his family, mainly, it has been said, because the presence of his own soldiers offered better security.

Eschewing limelight and controversy, Gowon was different in other respects. The media made a big thing about his having been trained in England at the Royal Military Academy, Sandhurst, as well as in Ghana. The truth, says Forsyth, "is that while it sounds like the full three-year permanent commission background, it was actually a three-month summer course which Commonwealth officers literally could not fail."

Gowon did get involved in two tours of duty with the Nigerian army during the Congo's upheavals and, by all accounts, did a sterling job in putting down some of the uprisings in the interior. And once the Biafran war had ended, it was General Yakubu Gowon who initiated the remarkable reconciliation that took place between the victors and the vanquished, in itself an astonishing gesture because it avoided unnecessary bloodshed. That this happened at a time when the Nigerian military clamoured to bring the entire Biafran command and their supporters to trial, made his efforts even more commendable,

The Enugu municipal offices as seen in 1959, a legacy of British colonialism.

Independence Square, Lagos, c. 1965. (Photo E. Ludwig)

The classically historic photo of the Sardauna of Sokoto and British officials at the independence review.

Lagos Lagoon.

Verdant jungle conditions in Biafra, tailor-made for ambushes. (Author's collection)

A street scene in a Biafran town during the war. Note the makeshift jungle camouflage on the red van.

A Biafran military vehicle parked in a street. (Author's photo)

Above left: Seen here in the Warri roadstead is the ship *Titania* that took several Biafran MiniCons rocket strikes. The author was on board at the time. (Author's collection)

Above right: After a Nigerian airstrike on a Biafran town, civilians rush to check for casualties.

Below: Improvised Biafran camouflage against MiG-17 attacks. (Author's photo)

A Biafran mortar unit being put through their paces. (Author's photo)

Biafran MiniCon pilot Jonny Cliukure.

Claymore mine ... Biafran style. (Author's photo)

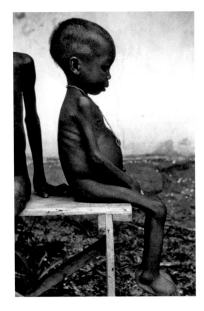

The iconic Biafran photo of a starving child.(Photo Dr Lyle Conrad)

Aid flights into Biafra begin.

Because of Nigerian aircraft, Biafran wounded could only be brought back for treatment by mammy wagon after dark. (Author's photo)

Ares Klootwyk in the cockpit of his Soviet MiG-17 (Ares Klootwyk collection)

Calabar was a major staging point for relief operations into Biafra.

A Biafran oil refinery after the war. Oil was of little strategic use to the Bifrans: the British and the Nigerians had it all neatly sewn up.

Biafran coffin transport during the war. (Photo Gilles Caron)

especially since there were those who wanted the lot executed. That Gowon managed to sidestep this bristlingly emotive issue underscores the measure of his resolve. After all, his opponents argued, hundreds of thousands of their own people's lives had been lost in what they regarded a senseless war.

Gowon had a ruthless—and some say, a sensible—side to him that went unheralded. He was the first African leader to hire foreign pilots to fight his war: first Egyptians to fly his Soviet jet fighters and bombers and then a batch of South African British, Australian and other mercenaries who were eventually to play a prime role in turning the war around.

At the same time, he was powerfully opposed to any direct humanitarian aid going into Biafra without the aircraft first landing at Nigerian airports to be checked. As a consequence, Gowon was implacably opposed to organizations like Oxfam and Joint Church Aid (cynically 'Jesus Christ Airlines'), which flew its planes into Biafra from the offshore Portuguese island colony of São Tomé.

In the political climate of an unstable Nigeria that was both unpredictable and volatile, General Gowon simply could not last. On a diplomatic mission to Uganda in July 1975, the Nigerian army deposed him. A few years later he enrolled at a British university as a student.

Forsyth: "Both the harsh and the gentle side of Gowon were deceptive because he was throughout like a glove puppet, either of the Fulani/Hausa zealots like Murtala Muhammed or the British advice which could spot a brilliant opportunity for good PR. Visiting correspondents and residents like Angus McDiarmid were constantly briefed by the high commissioner as if he were in total charge in all matters, when in reality, he was not."

Then came Aburi and the one crucial effort to prevent conflict. It was staged by the British high commissioner who held the post immediately before David Hunt, Sir Francis Coming-Bruce (known to the hack community as 'Cunning Brute'). All the parties were represented, with the intent of finding a compromise settlement and heading off secession and war.

Forsyth: "Ojukwu turned up at Aburi wholly focused and minutely briefed and he ended up running rings around the poor, floundering Gowon. The deal was nevertheless signed to general jubilation and relief."

But Lagos had made what were regarded as unwarranted concessions. The East was allowed to retain its federal taxes to cope with her almost two million penniless refugees who had fled the north and the west with only the clothes on their backs, leaving behind 30,000 dead and bringing with them the same number of machete-mutilated victims.

Forsyth: "Back in the capital afterwards, the northerners exploded and denounced the deal. The British High Commissioner briefed the press that Ojukwu had taken 'gross advantage' of the not-too-bright Gowon (who could have brought with him to Aburi a team of scholars of his own, but he chose to negotiate alone: Lagos then reneged on every point that had been agreed.)

"Ironically, accused by Sir David Hunt of being a dictator, Ojukwu was the only one of the two who bowed to the will of his people."

The Nigerian attitude, as we have seen, was 'good riddance' until London pointed out exactly where the oil lay.

Things were very different with regard to the other man in this complex political mix who was making things happen. After the tribal pogroms in the north, Lieutenant-Colonel Odumegwu Ojukwu emerged from the shadows almost as if it had been pre-ordained

There is still much debate—a good deal of it controversial—about the role of the individual whom I'd fleetingly known before the war and who took his people to war against the Federal government. Everybody kept a close watch on all these events, largely because having experienced two army mutinies, nobody wanted a third: they got a civil war instead. According to those close to the eastern military leader, and Frederick Forsyth in particular, his dismay was almost palpable as conditions started to deteriorate.

Colonel Ojukwu, an Oxford graduate, was outspoken about the long-term consequences of the killings. The nation was being irrevocably split, he chastised those involved in the original coup. Presciently, he warned that war might follow, if only because of the minority that were being persecuted and there was no question that something really drastic had to do done, if only to survive. Anything!

As he told Forsyth, the North was systematically trying to kill off his people. "If the atrocities do not stop, the Eastern Region will have to take appropriate action," was one of his public pronouncements. Similar sentiments were voiced shortly afterwards in a radio broadcast from Onitsha, the largest Ibo city in the east.

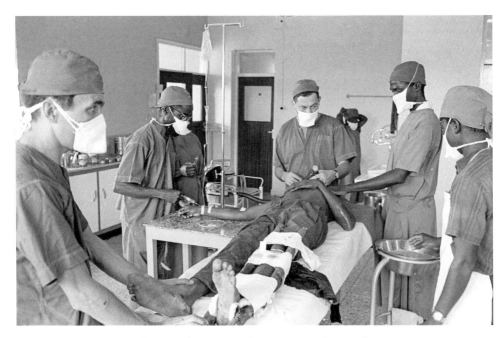

Doctors in Biafra worked under the most rudimentary conditions, here seen operating on a wounded soldier. (ICRC photo)

While Ojukwu always put the welfare of his people first, and ostensibly did not appear to be interested in the oil imbroglio that had started manifesting itself, the idea of seceding from the Nigerian Federation was already a hot issue in Enugu, because that city was the fulcrum on which just about everything of consequence in the eastern part of the country hinged.

Among the arguments that this Nigerian army colonel and his people liked to use, was that the boundaries of the country had been arbitrarily drawn by the British colonial government a century before, and, of course, he was right. Consequently, they maintained, original lines on the map of West Africa were of little use now.

At the same time, Ojukwu was the ultimate pragmatist. He told those around him that if it really became a matter of his people emerging from this mess with any kind of dignity, the newfound oil resource would play its role in giving the Ibo *nation* the economic power to go it alone. This was a situation much like that which prevailed in Rhodesia which had gone ahead and declared UDI in 1965. But in contrast to Biafra, Ian Smith had no oil reserves of his own, and he consequently paid the inevitable price.

Just about everybody in Lagos was aware at the time that Ojukwu had already sent his emissaries abroad to buy what weapons they could lay their hands on in Europe and the reaction was good. The word that came back was that France and several Eastern European countries were willing to sell guns, but it was all over-the-counter stuff, i.e. cash up front. The larger and more unsettling issue was getting that hardware back to Ojukwu's already-embattled enclave.

Paris, it should be mentioned, was motivated not so much by sympathy for an opposed or threatened African tribal group but by its own investments in Nigeria, many of which lay under the ground in the east of the country. Also, there were more French cars on Nigeria roads than those from any other nation, Britain and Japan included. Anybody who spent time in Nigeria after independence will recall the ubiquitous Peugeot taxis.

At about this point, things started to move rather quickly. Violence in the northern reaches of the country continued, though not as intensely as before because most easterners had fled. Also, killings in the Yoruba-dominated west abated markedly—though not nearly as widespread as in the north, a lot of others also died in the disturbances, including western Nigerians.

No fools, the Yoruba people were well aware by now that this was a largely Christian–Muslim thing, with the preponderant Islamic militants in the north doing what they could to cripple a largely Christian eastern Nigeria. That had a ripple effect on Nigerian society as a whole, and led to some germane questions being asked in Lagos and Ibadan: once the Ibos have been dealt with, are we likely to be next? The phrase 'Islamic jihad' was being bandied about by some as if this concept was already a reality.

So it came to pass that Nigeria's Eastern Region was declared the Republic of Biafra, its symbol the rising sun again a black backdrop.

Throughout this period, there was hardly a day when one or other Ojukwu pronouncement did not make news. Every newspaper in the country—including those in the north—had their journalists in the east and they reported the situation exactly as

Gowon was back by almost unlimited supplies of heavy artillery.

they saw it, though more often than not with strong emphasis on anything dramatic, like rumours of arms purchases abroad and once or twice, reports that white mercenaries had been hired to defend eastern borders. This was not the kind of thing that Lagos was likely to ignore.

One has to remember that the Congo and its hired guns were still fresh in the minds of most African people, not only in Nigeria but across the continent. Indeed, there was an argument doing the rounds that if Mobutu could use mercenaries to achieve victory, then so, in theory, might Ojukwu. In truth, it had not yet come to that.

Obviously the British played an increasingly devious role during this period, using its offices to unabashedly lend support to the Federal cause and view Ojukwu with great suspicion. It almost became a fetish within government circles to traduce the African leader, obviously because of the oil. I deal with this matter in some detail in the final chapter.

As the former colonial authority, there was regular contact with the East, but these meetings almost never went well or produced anything constructive. Also, Ojukwu had an ingrained suspicion about what Whitehall might come up with. More to the point, the biggest stumbling block was the high commissioner himself—who made no secret of the fact that he despised Ojukwu—and this sentiment went a good deal further than politics.

"Sir David's relations with Colonel Ojukwu were frosty," recalls Forsyth, one of the few observers active in Nigeria at the time that was either willing or able to spell it out. "The British High Commissioner, to be fair, was very much a product of the old British colonial establishment and he viewed black people in their proper place. Certainly, Ojukwu did not fit into that mould: he came with a British public school education and could actually be regarded as a black Englishman. He'd been to Oxford, played a good game of rugby, his father had been knighted by the King and was a self-made millionaire ... which meant of course that this was a man of substance."

Ojukwu, recalls Forsyth, regarded Sir David Hunt—university don, diplomat, author, archaeologist, TV personality and army officer—with the direst suspicion, "well-merited as it eventually turned out," he recalled.

"From the outset the British High Commissioner detested the Ibo military leader and the sentiment was thoroughly reciprocated ... On Hunt's part, there were two reasons. Unlike Ojukwu, the High Commissioner was not public school, despite the brilliant classical brain he demonstrated at Oxford. But he *was* a simply crashing snob and a covert racist. Two, he divorced his wife and married Iro Myrianthousis, the editor of *Lagos Weekly* and the favourite niece of the mega-rich, Lebanese-Greek, Nigerian-based tycoon A. G. Leventis ... What complicated matters here, was that Iro had been Emeka's [Ojukwu's] girlfriend, with the younger man vastly better endowed."

In his book *The Biafran War: The Struggle for Modern Nigeria*, Michael Gould, a British academic who had spent part of his youth in Nigeria, has his own views on the rebel leader.

He tells us that after several years of education at the Catholic Mission School followed by a spell at King's College in Lagos—one of the best educational establishments in West Africa and modelled on the British private school system—young Odumegwu was sent by his father to London. That was after Hitler's war had ended and he stayed as a house guest under the guardianship of John Whiter and his family. Ojukwu was educated first at Epsom College and then gained a place reading law at Lincoln College, Oxford. Forsyth mentioned that by then he was already aware that the legal profession was not for him, but for the sake of his father, Sir Louis, he stuck to it, filling in time by doing well in sports.

On his return to Nigeria, Gould continues, following interviews with Julia Burrows, "Ojukwu was almost able to claim by right of birth his position in the elite of Nigerian society, although, with due credit to him, he did not elect to join one of his father's companies where position, status and success would almost certainly have been guaranteed. Indeed, on one occasion in the Whiter household, he proclaimed that there would be uprisings and a war in Nigeria and that he would eventually become king, such was his confidence and arguably his arrogance."

Colonel Ojukwu addresses the nation.

Sir David Hunt never got on with the man he sometimes referred to as "that young upstart Ojukwu". In fact, quoting from FCO, Doc 25/232 held in the National Archives, Kew, he was astonishingly outspoken about the rebel colonel: "Power he has now got in full measure and he is obviously enjoying it; he also enjoys very much contemplating the superiority of his own intelligence and the lack of brains of the Head of the Federal Military Government and the other Regional Military Governors. If I had any confidence in my ability to tell character from appearance, I should say that there was some mental instability in him; apart from his appearance which there seems to be a touch of paranoia in the ease with which he believes unbelievable stories about the secret manoeuvres of his enemies."

Indeed, that was a rather unwarranted statement since it was an open secret that British intelligence was doing everything it could to discredit the Ibo leader, to the extent of even trying to find incriminating evidence in Frederick Forsyth's London apartment by illegally entering it while he was away and going through his things. Sir David would have been very much in the loop during the course of those Secret Intelligence Service machinations, though we are now also aware that Forsyth has been recruited by British SIS during this period.

Later, in the same document the British high commissioner goes on to say that he had met Odumegwu Ojukwu six years before as a young lieutenant "and I thought him polished and intelligent far beyond the average of the Nigerian officer".

Forsyth for his part, during many hours of taped recordings (as well as numerous off-the-cuff comments while we spent time together in Chinook, Washington) never uttered a disparaging word about the former Biafran leader whom he regarded as a close friend.

To the contrary, my immediate impression was that he really liked the man and after the civil war ended, the British author contributed liberally toward the education of Ojukwu's children once he had sought refuge in the Ivory Coast.

Though he did not elaborate, I got the impression that, as with other people that Frederick Forsyth helped when he began to make good money from his books, and Ojukwu got a share of it, so did some of the mercenaries who fought in Biafra and whom he'd befriended while there.

Obi Nwakanma, author of a treatise on Ojukwu, published in the Nigerian newspaper *Vanguard*, on 2 November 2003, made some interesting observations about young Ojukwu and I quote:

It is apparent that Chukwuemeka Odumegwu Ojukwu was driven by a sense of destiny. As a ten-year old boy in Form One at King's College in Lagos in 1943, he too had already joined the anti-colonial struggle. That year, he joined senior students like Anthony Enahoro and Ovie Whiskey, among others, to stage an anti-war, anti-colonial protest against the British administration, for which some of the students were reprimanded, others conscripted to fight, and from which people like Enahoro emerged into national limelight.

Ojukwu was tried as a juvenile in the courts in Lagos for his participation, and two pictures essay that moment: when he lay sleeping at the dock, and when his father, Sir Louis, carried him, still sleepy, on his shoulder at the end of proceedings. His radicalized consciousness was possibly sharpened when his father sent him off to school in England, to Epsom College, soon after the King's incident.

Black, stubborn, and opinionated, Ojukwu might have earned himself some unsavoury record. But he was a sportsman. He was brilliant. He was a rich boy. He was inevitable. In Oxford, Ojukwu joined the socialists, even though he rode about in a rather splendid Rolls Royce.

Wounded troops at Biafra's Okigwe hospital. (ICRC photo)

6. THE AIR WAR

On 30 May 1967 when the governor of the Eastern Region, Lieutenant-Colonel Odumegwu Ojukwu, announced a unilateral secession of the state of Biafra, it soon became apparent that there was a serious chance of Biafra managing to gain its independence, especially since a break from the Federal government was widely supported by the local population. The British were the first to realize that an independent Biafra could exploit the enormous resources of oil on which it lay. Additionally, it had access to a long stretch of coast with several ports.

Following the pogroms of the Islamic north in which thousands of easterners had been killed, Ojukwu not only envisaged secession, but had begun to prepare for it for quite some time. Unaware of his intentions, considerable Nigerian government funds were transferred into Swiss bank accounts to finance the new state.

As we now know, the Lagos junta was taken by surprise and it was not before the summer of 1967 that there was any significant reaction. Even then, it was thanks in the main

A British mercenary pilot flying MiGs for the Nigerian Air Force. (Ares Klootwyk photo)

to the direct or indirect involvement of foreign powers—foremost Great Britain and the USSR—that the central government became capable of starting a war against Biafra.

The Biafrans were swift to understand the importance of air power and to start organizing a rag-tag air force. Concurrently they used transport aircraft to bring supplies of weapons into the country. Regular flights of Air TransAfrica DC-7s from South Africa had been flying in since the summer of 1966 while still more operated from Portugal, using Portuguese Guinea (today Guiné-Bissau), as well as the Cameroon Republic as conduits.

In October 1966, for example, a Royal Air Burundi DC-4M Argonaut, flown by mercenary Henry Wharton/Heinrich Wartski, crash-landed at Garoua, in Cameroun with a load of army supplies from Rotterdam in the hold. The same pilot supposedly flew a Transportes Aereos Portugueses (TAP) Super Constellation into Malta where it was impounded with a load of weapons in September 1967.

Still more aircraft were subsequently involved, including several time-expired Constellations (some with bogus Nigerian registrations like 5N83H, 5N84H, and 5N86H), DC-4s, DC-6s, and an Air TransAfrica DC-7 (VP-WBO/ZP-WBO), flown by Ernest Koenig, the Rhodesian Jack Malloch, and British mercenary Alistair Wickes.

On 23 April 1967 a Nigerian Airways Fokker F-27 was hijacked while underway from Benin to Lagos, and forced to land in Enugu. A colour photo shows this aircraft after it arrived at Enugu airport, then still the Biafran capital. The plane was later rejigged as makeshift bomber.

A second transport, a DC-3 of Ghana Airways was added on 15 June, after being hijacked from Port Harcourt.

From early July an ex-French Douglas B-26R Invader went operational from Enugu after being delivered to Biafra by Polish World War II flying ace Jean Zumbach (also known as Johnny Brown or Kamikaze Braun).

Another B-26 followed that August. By then an American- registered Riley Dove was delivered to Biafra from Switzerland with André Juillard/Girard/Gerard at the controls. It had on board 2.000 Hungarian-manufactured rifles. The aircraft was subsequently pushed into a reconnaissance role, but a short while later was forced down inside Algeria and impressed into service with that country's air force.

The Federal army began mobilizing on 6 July 1967 and initiated hostilities a few days later by securing the towns Ogoja, Nsukka, and the oil terminal at Bonny. The Biafran Air Force (BiAF) struck back within days, sending its aircraft to bomb the airfield at Makurdi where several civilian DC-3s—used for the transport of Federal troops—were damaged.

Later the same week the remaining B-26R was used to strike Lagos and Kano, but the raids caused only slight damage, principally because the Nigerian Air Force (NAF)—still not properly operational—had few targets static on the ground.

On 26 July the B-26 and the hijacked DC-3 were used to attack the frigate NNS *Nigeria* which had been tasked with blockading Biafra's largest serviceable harbour, Port Harcourt. Earlier, after the second B-26 arrived in Biafra, both Invaders were used to attack and sink a large passenger ferry which operated services across the Niger river.

A Czech-built Delphin fighter-trainer that flew for the NAF.

With the Biafrans all but uncontested in the air, Lagos was desperate to obtain the kind of combat aircraft which could be deployed to retaliate. After brief negotiations with the Soviet Union as well as Great Britain, the USSR started delivering the first MiG-17s, ferried by air from Egypt to Kano on 13 August 1967. More were sent by sea from the Eastern Bloc. Sudan lent Nigeria two Jet Provosts, but these were soon inoperable.

The BiAF reacted with a series of strikes against Kano, on 19 and 20 August, destroying several newly arrived MiG-17s on the ground. It is worth mentioning that the Biafrans lacked conventional bombs, and made do very successfully with improvised ordnance, Nevertheless, the MiGs became operational and flew their first combat sorties soon afterwards, attacking the Onitsha airfields.

The NAF achieved its first success on 10 September when the MiGs destroyed one of the B-26s on the ground at Enugu. The arrival of the first squadron of Soviet MiG-17 jets changed not only the situation in the air, but their presence was soon to be felt on the ground as well.

In a large offensive, on 22 September the Biafrans were pushed out of Benin City, and in the following days they lost more ground: Enugu fell on 4 October, and Ojukwu was forced to move his capital to Umuahia. On 7 October 1967, Biafra's lone Fokker F-27 was lost over Lagos: Federal troops claimed that they had shot it down but far more likely it crashed following the premature detonation of one of the makeshift bombs in its hold.

During the following winter, bad weather and an acute lack of spares on both sides made flying almost impossible, but by May both sides were back in the air and Federal forces had started a new offensive.

Port Harcourt fell on 18 May, with the BiAF losing its lone DC-3 as well as another B-26. At the time the Biafrans and their mercenaries attempted to acquire jets as well, purchasing two Fouga Magisters from Austria. But, while the fuselages of the 4D-YF and 4D-YL arrived intact, their wings were sabotaged while in Bissau, leaving them useless.

The Federal offensive continued, and on 18 June 1968 Awgu fell, leaving Biafra with only a single airstrip, a stretch of a strengthened road near Uli-Ihailia, named 'Annabelle'. The Red Cross was in the process of constructing another airstrip near Afikpo. This strip was to be used not only by C-97Gs of the ICRC, but also DC-4s and C-130s employed by both the French and Swedish Red Cross organizations. Still more aircraft chartered by Joint Church Aid and the World Council of Churches from Balair (two DC-6As), as well as many others—including smaller relief organizations, mainly flying ex-RAF Ansons, to haul food and medical supplies—used the improvised air strips. By November 1968 roughly twenty tonnes of food and supplies were flown into Biafra on average just about every night they were functional.

The West German government even released the third prototype Transall C-160 to Balair: the aircraft flew 198 missions from Cotonou in Dahomey (Benin) in 1969.

An Egyptian Air Force Il-28 Beagle bomber sent to Nigeria to fly for the NAF.

The NAF, meanwhile, was not only operating MiG-17s, but six Ilyushin Il-28 bombers—flown by Egyptian and Czech pilots—that were delivered from Egypt and stationed at Calabar and Port Harcourt. The aircraft were deployed on numerous raids which not only damaged both airstrips in Biafra, but also struck at many other installations as well as towns of no military significance. Within months they had killed over 2,000 civilians.

With the NAF able to maintain almost complete air superiority, flights within the rebel territory by foreign-registered transport planes by day became extremely hazardous: everything had to be done at night.

During this phase, Ojukwu managed to arrange enough mercenaries to fly into Biafra from abroad to organize the 4th Commando Brigade, which was to become the leading unit in the following offensive on Onitsha. It also encircled the 3rd Nigerian Commando Division at Owerri and caused serious losses.

The NAF attempted to resupply this besieged garrison as well as the 3rd Division from the air, but eventually both towns were captured by Biafrans. This resulted in General Gowon being forced—under immense pressure from his advisers as well as the British, because of enormous negative publicity abroad of the starving millions—to find ways of enabling relief aircraft to continue operations into Biafra, while trying to filter arms supplies. An acceptable solution was never found and the weapons-flow into the rebel enclave continued right until the end. This, in turn, enabled a new development in the war.

In late 1968 and early 1969 the World Council of Churches was flying supplies to Biafra aboard several Transair DC-7Bs, one of which was piloted by the Swede Count Carl Gustav von Rosen. Greatly concerned about the plight of the Biafrans, he returned home in a bid to form a new Biafran air force unit by purchasing five MFI-9B MiniCon armed trainers. At the same time, he contracted several mercenaries to fly the machines. The MiniCons were shipped to France, to be armed with unguided rockets, and then to Libreville, to be assembled and camouflaged. The new Biafran 'fighters' became operational at Orlu, on 22 May 1969.

On the same day one of them was used to attack the Port Harcourt airfield, where two MiG-17s and two Il-28s were claimed destroyed or damaged. Two days later the tiny MiniCons attacked Benin City airfield, damaging a MiG-17 and an Ilyushin Il-28. On 28 May Enugu was hit, and in the following night part of Port Harcourt's oil installations were rocketed and went up in flames.

Von Rosen returned to Sweden to acquire more MiniCons, allegedly for the Abidjan Flying Club, but these did not to arrive until October.

Meanwhile Ernest Koenig bought two former West German C-47s for Colonel Ojukwu's air force and in November 1969, four AT-6 Texans were acquired. On 9 November the T-6s hit Port Harcourt airfield and claimed destruction of a Pan African Airways DC-4.

In response, the NAF started flying combat air patrols over the area; one of the British mercenaries flying a MiG-17 claimed that one of the AT-6s was shot down. In the same month a Fred Olsen Line DC-6 crashed at Uli while attempting to land at night.

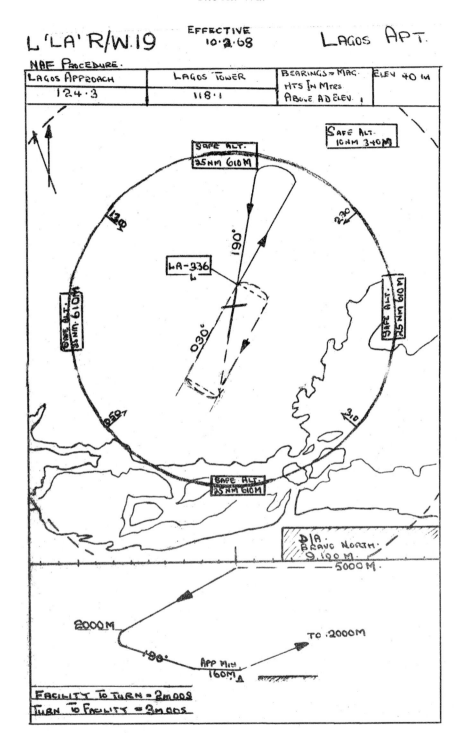

A flight plan filed at Lagos Ikeja airport during the war. (Author's photo)

Dateline Enugu, Eastern Nigeria, November 1968

Nigerian Air Force MiG 619 was one of the MiG-17Fs supplied as a part of the third batch to reach Nigeria between 12 October and 4 November 1968. It operated from Benin, Enugu as well as Port Harcourt as part of the 2nd Fighter-Bomber Squadron and is known to have been flown by a British mercenary pilot who earned £1,000 a month. The first six MiG-17Fs supplied by the Soviets all arrived on board Soviet AN-12 transports, with more coming into Lagos from Eastern Europe by ship.

Despite some of the blows inflicted by the Biafran MiniCons, the Federal forces were gradually succeeding in isolating the rebel state from the world outside. The country was being starved into submission.

In June 1969 a Red Cross DC-7 crashed after crossing the coast near Eket, after being attacked by a MiG-17, flown by a British contract pilot.

Ojukwu immediately attempted to acquire night-fighters. He settled for a pair of Meteor NF.14s, used by Templewood Aviation as target-towing aircraft by Enterprise Films. While both fighters reached Africa, the first ended its mission by being seized by the Portuguese authorities after it landed to refuel in Bissau, Portuguese Guinea. The other was reported missing on 10 November 1969 off the Cape Verde Islands but the Dutch pilot was rescued.

On 22 December 1969 Federal troops—supported by MiG-17s and Il-28s—launched the final offensive against the rebel state, cutting the territory under control by Ojukwu in half. Three weeks later, on 13 January 1970 all remaining Biafran forces capitulated: Colonel Ojukwu escaped from Uli to Abidjan, in the Ivory Coast aboard Super Constellation 5N-86H.

There he was welcomed and given sanctuary by Ivoirian president Félix Houphouët-Boigny.[*]

An Ace Mercenary Aviator Flies Soviet MiGs

There are few of the 'older generation' aviators who served in both the South African Air Force (SAAF) and the Royal Air Force (RAF) who can claim the distinction of having fought as a mercenary aviator in several irregular campaigns in Africa as well as the Middle East. Ares Klootwyk, a veteran of five different air forces, has done all that and more. He started his 'unconventional' flying after being hired as a mercenary in the Congo where he flew T-6 Texans, T-28 Trojans and Douglas A26s. He moved on to helicopters and fighter jets in Nigeria and was the first Western pilot to climb into the cockpit of a Soviet MiG-17.

Before that, after service with the SAAF where he flew Harvard T-6s and converted to British-built Vampire jets, then Dakotas and Lockheed Venturas, he headed off to London,

---

[*] With thanks to Tom Cooper for this section.

Above: Loading
food supplies
onto a Red
Cross chartered
aircraft. (ICRC
photo)

Right: Nigerian
Air Force
Ilyushin bomber
that landed short
at Port Harcourt.

ending up with the rank of flight lieutenant in the RAF. Sent off to RAF Lincolnshire on a fifty-hour refresher course—on the Percival Provost, a British basic trainer—he was dispatched to RAF station Bahrain in the Persian Gulf where he flew seven-passenger, high-winged, twin-engine Percival Pembrokes as well as STOL Twin Pioneers.

His career in the Gulf lasted two years, with 152 Transport Squadron at the RAF station in Bahrain and other postings to Kuwait, Oman and the United Arab Emirates. While based at Salalah in Oman, he was thrown headlong into developments in nearby Yemen and frequently had to ferry SAS elements (British and Rhodesian) as well as Trucial Oman Scouts for clandestine desert operations in the interior. At the time, Oman was suffering a low-grade insurgency sparked by Yemeni rebel tribes. The British army and the Royal Marines had been in Oman off and on to protect the Sultanate from tribal rebellions and invasions. The RAF was heavily involved, as was the RRAF, the Royal Rhodesian Air Force

In June 1964, having spent five years away from South Africa, he returned and on reaching Johannesburg, read a story in the Johannesburg *Star* that mercenaries—pilots included—were being recruited for active military service in the Congo, then in turmoil.

From the Congo, Klootwyk went straight into Nigeria's war against the recalcitrant Biafrans, a year-long episode of his life that he regards as among the most interesting and stimulating, especially since he was the first Western pilot to take one of Moscow's MiG-17s aloft. That aircraft was then still a relatively unknown factor for Americans combat pilots in Vietnam.

There is no question that the Soviet Mikoyan-Gurevich MiG-17 (NATO codenamed 'Fresco') was an outstanding aircraft. It did everything expected of it during the course of the Vietnam War: the Americans lost something like seventy of their planes in aerial combat to them.

Even though considered obsolete by the mid-1960s—and denigrated by many Western aviation experts—this stubby, swept-wing jet fighter was able to give an excellent account of itself in aerial combat against the North American F-100 Super Sabre. Only recently has it been disclosed that in South East Asia the MiG-17 was secretly flown in combat by Soviet aviators, and that it became the favourite combat fighter of most top North Vietnamese pilots, including that country's leading ace, the appropriately named Colonel Tomb.

Because the MiG-17 played such an important role in air operations against the Biafrans in their thirty-month West African conflict, it is important to fully appreciate exactly what this versatile little flying machine could do.

The prototype MiG-17 first flew in January 1950 and was reported to have exceeded Mach 1 in level flight with a normal ceiling close to 60,000 feet. It weighed in at about 13,400 pounds, or 6,090kg (maximum takeoff weight) and was armed with two 23 mm cannons as well as a single 37 mm cannon.[*] Pilots flying these jets in Nigeria rarely fired

---

[*] By comparison, the weapons capacity, alone, of today's F/A-18 Hornet, the United States twin-engine supersonic carrier-capable combat jet, is 20,000 pounds.

the cannon because it was regarded as slow and had a poor trajectory. While the MiG-17 packed a mighty punch in its air-to-air combat capabilities, the jet was even more effective when unopposed. It roamed Biafran skies at will, constantly in search of targets of opportunity. These included vehicles on the roads, Biafran military emplacements, troops on the move and, without fail, Count Carl Gustav von Rosen's elusive little Swedish MiniCons that could pack an inordinately powerful punch, though the trouble for those flying NAF planes was finding them

Whichever way the pilots turned within the enclave, there was always something for the Nigerian jets to attack. Travelling about Biafra by road, we were particularly vulnerable and had to keep a constant watch for anything in the air that might be threatening, MiGs especially.

An interesting aside here is the fact that Biafran casualties were never moved to medical dressing stations during daylight hours: they did not dare to because of the MiGs. The wounded always had to wait until dark before the trucks could trundle out of their jungle hiding places. Had they not done so, they would have become easy targets. The result was that anyone who suffered a gut wound in that tropical heat, was usually dead within six or eight hours from septicaemia.

To Klootwyk, Nigeria, following his Congolese deployments, was a revelation:

"What emerged after I'd got there was that that country was in serious need of professional pilots, both for helicopters (which I'd flown in the Congo and the RAF) as well as fixed-wing planes. Also, it was pleasing to be told that my salary would be paid in any

Nigerian Air Force spotter plane (Author's photo)

currency and into any bank in the world. Essentially, for us guys, it was very much a win–win situation: the added bonus was that Biafra had no fighter aircraft of its own.

"The deal was basic. We worked five months on, with a month off on full pay, together with a return ticket back to where we had originally come from. Or the equivalent amount toward any other destination of choice. The small print that each one of us signed indicated conditions while on operations and included a life insurance policy if we were killed or wounded. From the start, we were housed at good hotels and fed three meals a day. The downside was that we had to pay for our drinks, which was perhaps just as well because some of the fellows would have drunk the bars dry had they been given the choice."

He disclosed too, that individual pilots were able to take their wives, mistresses or girl-friends to Nigeria, also paid for by the Nigerians—return tickets, accommodation, food and all—with everything supplied by the government. The women were even allowed to accompany their men as far as Port Harcourt.

There were approximately sixteen mercenary pilots hired by the NAF over the duration of the war, comprised mainly of British, South African, French, Australian, Polish and possibly one or two more nationalities as the war progressed. At any period there were perhaps five to eight active pilots on contract.

"I arrived at Lagos's Ikeja Airport on 11 January 1968. I was met by Yorkie Grimes, a former British serviceman who had Royal Navy helicopter technical experience and whose

The Nigerian Airways Fokker 27 hijacked by Biafrans and later used to bomb Lagos.

day job was to look after Nigerian Air Force helicopters. We weren't issued uniforms and always wore civvies, except that we donned overalls for flying. Just about everything that happened in that West African nation was fairly haphazard and unplanned," Klootwyk admits. "Like the thirty minutes of dual-instruction I was given on a Westland Whirlwind Mark II helicopter after the Nigerians acquired eight from the Austrian Air Force. Immediately afterwards I was posted to the air base at Makurdi in northern Nigeria on general duties. But then this was Africa and you went along with it because you were expected to make things happen, something we were all pretty good at."

Because the Soviets were involved in Nigeria in support of the Lagos war effort against the Biafrans, it is axiomatic that Klootwyk would have had contact with what, until a short time before, in the Cold War context, had been potential enemies. He had served in the RAF and was clearly well aware of the implications of mixing with those with dubious agendas, though obviously his clandestine links with both British and American intelligence officers in Nigeria served a useful purpose. Others regarded him as bit of a 'curiosity piece', especially since he was South African and had flown combat in the Congo.

Before Klootwyk went to Nigeria, a large group of Egyptians had arrived in the country to provide support for the war. They flew MiGs and their Ilyushin-28 bombers and handled maintenance. But, says Klootwyk, it was obvious from the start that the Nigerians were not impressed by these Middle Eastern aviators. They were rarely prepared to take chances, going in on bombing raids against Biafran targets at high altitudes which was stupid because the Biafrans had hardly any ammunition. Consequently, said Klootwyk, the timid Arabs had "piss-poor results.

"Then somebody at Air Force Headquarters in Lagos got the idea that it might be a good idea to get some of us involved with the MiGs. The Egyptians were pretty useless, so this could only be an improvement, and anyway, most of us already had good combat experience with fighters: it was a natural progression."

In October 1969, eight Soviet Antonov-12s each delivered a single MiG-17 to Kano International Airport, the so-called 'MiG-17 Glatt' from East Germany because that country was retiring its MiG-17As from service."

The 'Glatt' definition emerged from 'gloss pipe' (in German), which indicated these jets were not equipped with afterburners. According to Klootwyk, the first problem to be faced was that Moscow was never keen on supplying MiG-17s to the NAF: "We mercenaries were actually the problem, because most of us had served in the RAF and other Western Bloc air forces. The Soviets were actually dead set against us getting anywhere near their planes, in large part because the operating parameters of the MiG-17 were still secret.

"By then Jimmy Webb, another British pilot, and I were already active against the Biafrans. We were flying armed Czech L-29 Delfins and the day came when we were quietly told by our Nigerian commander that we were to fly MiGs—obviously very much against the wishes of the Soviets.

"The two of us were ordered up to Kano to meet our instructors. Mine was Major Jibrin, a Nigerian Air Force pilot and Jimmy had an Egyptian put him through his paces. Our conversion consisted of three flights each in tandem dual-seat MiG-15s: total dual

One of a handful of T-6s to reach Biafra during the war.

instruction time of about a hundred minutes. A fifteen-minute solo flight on a MiG-17 followed. Easy enough, we thought when Jimmy and I compared notes afterwards. That was followed later by a thirty-minute instruction in Soviet gunnery procedures on one of the Mi-15s. It consisted of going in fast on a ground attack and firing our machine guns and the jet's cannon. We then did a further forty-five minutes general flying and an hour of gunnery practice on the MiG-17 before returning to Lagos and on to Benin where were made fully operational. It was one of the quickest conversions sessions I'd seen any pilot undergo, but being young, we were quick to learn."

Klootwyk explained that the MiG-17 had a conventional cockpit layout, except that the instruments and cockpit instructions were in Cyrillic script and the instruments were marked in kilometres-per-hour and in metres: "After a simple pre-flight routine, we discovered that the MiG had very good visibility, was an easy starter and simple to taxi—as against the RAF Vampire which had similar brake and peddle actuation but was more difficult to control.

"My first take-off in dual MiG-15 was a cinch, but with such superior performance to the L-29—which I'd been flying until then—I found myself at 300 metres before I remembered to retract the undercarriage, such was its superior thrust. Airborne handling was no problem and neither of us encountered any difficulty in touch-and-go or full-stop landings.

"After three short flights with Major Jibrin, I soloed on the MiG-17 and notably, I found no real superior performance compared to the MiG-15. What the MiG-17 did have was

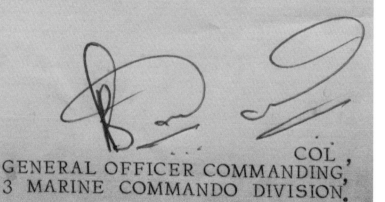

Memorandum

From GOC

04 MAY *19*69

To.......... Capt Alfa ....

....

Go on the farm settlement furing
your second sortie. You will go on
the Ohekelem - Olakwo run. Fire
the Houses. They are all in there.

Our own tps are in Okpuala. The
en are now in Objs 1 to 4. They are
your tgets.

Serious attacking going on now.
Hurry.

COL ,
GENERAL OFFICER COMMANDING,
3 MARINE COMMANDO DIVISION.

Operational orders for NAF pilots to strike at Biafran positions: brief and snappy.
(Author's photo)

a good rate of climb, coupled to easy handling and landing. It was an excellent fighting machine. On our operations over Biafra there was never any need—unless ferrying an aircraft—to go above 3,000 feet as our operations were mainly ground attack. Flight time on internal tanks was no more than forty minutes, and with two drop tanks of 100 gallons each, we could remain aloft up to eighty minutes.

"We also found that the aircraft's 23mm machine guns were effective since every third round or so was a tracer, which meant that you could easily remain visually on target. The 37mm cannon in contrast was disappointing. We hardly ever used it because of the unsatisfactory trajectory of its shell, which one could see dropping practically the moment it left the barrel." There were rarely any glitches when handling the MiGs operationally, says Klootwyk.

The Nigerians used a variety of ploys to harass the Biafrans, one of the more effective being nighttime raids over rebel airstrips in which one of their Dakotas was converted to drop improvised bombs and incendiary devices. Some transport pilots landing at Uli, Uga and other strips referred euphemistically to the aircraft as 'Intruder'; others used harsher language.

Klootwyk and his fellow pilots had little contact with these unconventionally minded mercenaries, who soon acquired a reputation, if not for accuracy, then for a measure of ruthlessness.

For much of the war the focus of Klootwyk and his colleagues was fixed on Biafra's Uli airstrip where Nigeria's mercenary pilots always experienced ground fire, usually when they arrived in the morning to see what aircraft had been left behind overnight. That would happen if a plane couldn't take off because of unserviceability or mishaps, like being hit by 'friendly' ground fire when landing (which happened) or possibly bomb damage from the NAF DC-3 which arrived over the airstrip just about every night.

"The tactics we used with the MiGs was for the leader to come in at about 400 mph in a left-hand circuit and at an altitude of roughly 1,000 feet. Number Two would follow about ten seconds later. We'd have quite a bit of reaction from the ground—usually ack-ack and machine-gun fire toward the first aircraft, but with no offset for speed. The rounds would burst and traverse between the two jets and the second plane would then dive down and fire on the enemy position which would immediately be silenced.

"After that we would pretty well have carte blanche to take out any other targets on the airstrip. Yet, looking back, we must have been quite lucky because we were never really hit. The only casualties we experienced were when Biafran MiniCons and Harvards attacked our planes on the airfields from where we operated: as compact as those tiny planes were, they sometimes caused some serious damage."

There was no question that the NAF MiG-17s soon became a significant factor in the internecine war being waged in West Africa. Reports that subsequently emerged, suggest that the Soviet planes made a significant change to rebel tactics, in large part because almost all movement on the enclave's roads during daylight hours were halted.

While flown by Egyptian pilots neither the MiGs nor the Ilyushin IL-28 bombers made much difference. They bombed and strafed as required of them, but always at altitude, while the mercenary aviators in Lagos's pay preferred the low, fast and accurate option. One of the more significant advantages displayed by the Soviet fighter jets was that they were fitted with heavy-duty landing gear designed to be used on rough or poorly prepared landing strips and reflected solid, rugged aluminium construction throughout. As a result, the MiG-17 could be easily maintained in the field by ground crews.

Klootwyk remembers that most maintenance problems on the Soviet jets could be fixed with pretty basic equipment and ordinary tools, very different from Western aircraft which often needed entire workshops to achieve results. Consequently, by the time he and Jimmie Webb climbed into the cockpit of this 'still unknown' aircraft in Lagos for the first time, Western intelligence agencies were very much on the tails of both aviators, eager to get their views not only on how this Soviet fighter performed, but also in the hopes that they might be able to pinpoint some of its shortcomings.

"Though it took a bit of time, we didn't disappoint either the Americans or the British," Klootwyk is happy to confirm today.

Obviously, Biafra's MiniCons were simply no match when facing the MiGs: the jets were simply too fast and sophisticated for the little prop-driven jobs that usually flew only metres above the jungle. Klootwyk recalls a run-in with the MiniCons, though he was on the ground at the time: "We were all at Port Harcourt when several of those little fighters staged their first attack and they caught just about everybody by complete surprise. I was having a snooze after lunch in the airport hotel when a series of strange popping

Port Harcourt bustled with Nigerian aircraft after it had been taken. (Ares Klootwyk photo)

sounds woke me. I went to my balcony from which I could see the airport and in a befuddled state I thought I saw an aircraft about the size of a Cessna-150 buzzing around the airfield. It didn't really register just then that we were under attack so I went back to bed.

"Only then did I become aware of what was actually taking place. I took another look outside to confirm my fears, got dressed, phoned another of our pilots and told him to meet me outside as soon as possible. Something very strange was happening at the airfield, I said. We jumped into one of our Mini-Mokes, drove to the airfield and found one of the AfricAir DC-4 freighters on fire at the terminal. We then went to our hangar where there were more fires, including one of our jets burning with gusto. The enemy MiniCons had gone by then, but the damage these little planes inflicted was remarkable considering that they weighed only a few hundred kilos.

"Another time we were having lunch in the hotel when I heard a sound of an aircraft that was quite familiar because I'd originally trained on them. It was a T-6 Harvard approaching the airport at a very low level. When it passed over the hotel it fired a long machine-gun burst which we later learned was at a truck in the road below and which killed the driver. It disappeared pretty sharply after that and we couldn't find it after we'd scrambled."

The MiniCon

Among foreigners involved in this bloody internecine conflict, there were other others who did not 'turn a coin'. Count Gustav von Rosen created what he liked to believe was an 'instant air force' for the near-planeless Biafra during one of his summer vacations. He didn't charge a penny for his services.

A MiG-17 crash-landed in the bush at Port Harcourt: it ran out of fuel. (Ares Klootwyk photo)

When he flew his squadron of second-hand MFI-9B Swedish trainers into Biafra from Gabon, they were so heavily loaded with extra fuel tanks, rockets in wing-pods and radio equipment that some of the aviators who were there said the planes wouldn't make it all the way across that long stretch of ocean between Gabon and Nigeria. But they did, and within a day or two their pilots notched up their first strikes.

In the first three raids after arriving in the rebel territory, these modest little 'fighters'—flown mostly by mercenaries but with good Biafran backup—bagged several NAF aircraft in a succession of strikes on airports at Benin City and Port Harcourt. The tally included a MiG-17 as well as an Egyptian Air Force Ilyushin-28—all blasted while still on the ground.

After that, Biafran pilots had to be a lot more circumspect: there were any number of NAF planes—including MiGs—out looking for them and their hiding places in the jungle.

As 'fighters' go, the 'MiniCons' were among the smallest modern combat aircraft built. 'Von Rosen's Vengeance'—as the modest prop-driven little planes were called by the media—proved astonishingly effective.

One blogger, who calls himself 'Srbin' (all we know about him is that he was born in 1986) commented that "even the Skyraider was like an SR-71 compared to the little putt-putt plane around which Von Rosen built his force: the tiny Swedish trainer looked like those ultra-lights that people build in their garages. This plane could park in sub-compact

A MiG-17 abandoned on a runway after landing. (Ares Klootwyk photo)

spaces at one of Stockholm's shopping malls ... it had a maximum payload of 500 pounds" or, as he said, "me plus a couple of medium-sized dogs ... in Gabon, Von Rosen slapped on a coat of green VW paint to make them look military and on each aircraft, he installed twin wing pods for French-built Matra 68mm unguided rockets. Then he and his pilots—three Swedish volunteers who took time off from their civilian jobs, together with three Nigerians—flew them back to Biafra. This unlikely septet immediately went into combat, the next day. More MiniCons were bought later, again paid for by this Swedish aristocrat."

Srbin again: "They blew the hell out of the Nigerian Air Force as well as the Nigerian Army. These little fleas were impossible to bring down. Not one was knocked out of the sky, although they'd buzz home, sometimes riddled with holes. They often flew three missions a day and their list of targets destroyed included Nigerian airfields, power plants, and troop concentrations.

"Caught napping on the ground, they also knocked out two, possibly three Soviet MiG-17 jet fighters (and damaged another two); one Ilyushin-28; a British-built Canberra bomber (as well as one more damaged); the 'Intruder' (the twin-engine DC-3 transport plane manned by the South African mercenary who called himself 'Genocide' and who would bomb civilian aid aircraft as they landed in the dark), as well as two helicopters, with one more damaged.

"That was hardly a bad tally for a rebel air force that the Lagos government—throughout two-and-a-half years of hostilities—routinely declared 'did not exist'," declared Srbin.

At one stage, in a bid to supplement his MiniCons, the Biafran leader bought several World War II-surplus T-6 Harvards, but they were in a poor condition because only four were airworthy. During their initial transit flight from Gabon to Biafra, two were lost. The remaining pair was used in strikes, usually in conjunction with the MFI-9Bs—the Malmö Flygindustri MFI-9 Junior—nine of which by then were still in service. During the latter part of the war, two MiniCons were destroyed, presumably by ground fire, which could sometimes be intense.

Interestingly, Artur Alves Pereira, a Portuguese mercenary pilot—at one stage, a Portuguese Air Force squadron leader in that country's colonial wars—flew T-6s as well as MiniCons for Biafra. He was the last freelance pilot to fly out of the beleaguered enclave on 9 January 1970 and was dropped off in Gabon.

From there, he headed home to Lisbon and although the war was over and all rebel offices in Portugal were closed, the now non-existent Biafran government sent him a final pay cheque which covered all the war missions he had flown, as he told friends, "down to the last penny." He commented afterwards that this small example showed how "special a people the Igbo [Ibos] are ... Which country in the world, let alone in Africa, would bother to fulfil its commitments to this extent? Which messenger wouldn't feel tempted to keep part, or even all of the money?" The amount he received, he admits, "was quite a lot at that time, especially when the future seemed so uncertain to everybody involved." Obviously, he concluded, there would have been no court to which to complain.

Another significant comment was that with experience gathered over time at the 'sharp end', the tiny MiniCons, in true guerrilla style, turned their weaknesses—small size and low speed—to their own effective advantage. They were so slow that they simply *had* to

MiG-17 details penned by Klootwyk during a debrief (Author photo)

fly really low—which made them almost impossible to hit in the jungle, since you never saw them until they were almost on top of you. This made for better aiming capability than the sleeker and faster MiGs: almost half of the roughly 400 rockets the MiniCons

An NAF MiG-17. (Ares Klootwyk photo)

fired hit their targets, which is an amazing tally for unguided aircraft munitions. Clearly, these minuscule MFI-9Bs packed a decisive punch.

Apart from the Harvards, there was also a surplus World War II American-built bomber which had mixed fortunes before it crashed after a raid over Nigerian lines. After the war ended, a BiAF de Havilland DH-104 Riley Dove emerged. It was discovered in wrecked condition on the playing fields of a school in Uli. Tom Cooper told me that this was bit of a revelation as the authorities were only aware that a single Dove—a US-registered Riley Dove—was delivered to Port Harcourt from Switzerland after having been impounded for a while in Algeria in the summer of 1967.

Though the MiniCons were active for more than a year, few of those involved in the war—except pilots flying for the Nigerians—have recorded their impressions of coming under attack by them. I was, en route to Biafra on a freighter that had stopped at the Nigerian port of Warri in the Niger Delta. I was in my cabin on board the Swedish merchantman *Titania* when the first salvo struck: two powerful blasts in quick succession. It was like a car backfiring, only up close. The impact of exploding rockets reverberated throughout the ship and my immediate impulse was to get myself up top. Two, three steps at a time, I shot up the companionway and emerged on deck, just in time to spot two small single-engine aircraft turning low on the water about five or six hundred metres away. These were the dreaded MiniCons of course, and in any other circumstance the attack would have been regarded as a stroke of luck. We were only to find out afterwards that the planes had that morning scored their first major strike against maritime targets in the Nigerian civil war. Just then, they were heading straight back at us. Two more spurts of smoke from their underwing pods told me all I needed to know. I'd seen enough war movies to be aware that more rockets were heading our way. There was no thinking about it: my only option was to hurl myself down the same companionway from which I had just emerged. Moments later more blasts erupted behind the bulkhead, one of them about two metres above my head. For a second or two I had the air knocked of me and it took a little while to get back on my feet. Meanwhile, another projectile hit the ship amidships and then one more above the waterline. Whoever was using these things knew what they were doing.

Though neutral, the Scandinavian merchant ship which I boarded as a passenger in Tema, Ghana had suddenly become a casualty. So had the American steamer moored ahead of us in Warri's roadstead. Both freighters had made their way the fifty or so kilometers up the estuary of West Africa's biggest river and found themselves caught in a conflict that was already into its third year. Comparatively speaking, the *Titania*—the ship I'd boarded the week before and which was taking me to Douala in the Cameroons—had come off lightly. Not so the *African Crescent*, then in the final stages of a West African run out of Houston. Though there were larger-than-usual Stars and Stripes hanging fore and aft, she also sported a Farrell Lines crest on her smoke stack. Two of its crew members were killed and seven wounded.

Only afterwards was I able to put together some of it. Having watched the MiniCons do their turn over the river and fire a second salvo, I'd thrown myself down the same narrow set of stairs from which I'd emerged a short while before and in the process landed slap-bang on top of two female members of the ship's crew making their way up. The three of us collapsed in a heap at the foot of the companionway. The rocket that had detonated nearest us exploded in the ship's linen cupboard, immediately under the stairs behind us. A year's supply of sheets, blankets and towels absorbed most of the blast and we weren't hurt, though my ears zinged for a week afterwards.

Biafran MiniCon crews wait for orders.

Count von Rosen in a bush bar in Biafra.

It was an eventful morning for everybody. Having gone into action against us at Warri, the MiniCons pulled away and banked toward one of four of five tiny airstrips where fortified concrete bunkers had been built deep inside Biafra, but not before they struck again at several oil storage tanks on the outskirts of the port, sending plumes of black smoke into the air. By then two merchant ships were dousing their fires and I was taking pictures.

Though damage was real and there had been casualties, as far as the Nigerian government was concerned, it never happened. Nor, insisted the Federal government spokesman, were a million Biafran children starving. And since I was stringing for the London *Daily Express* and this was an event that needed to get out, I was faced with the dilemma of trying to communicate the news from a country at war. No, said the captain, his ship was neutral and he could not, or rather, *would not* allow his radio officer to send 'war reports' from the *Titania*. I countered with another request: what about *me* transmitting the copy? I'd done a spell of telegraphy in the navy and suggested that I could push it out to one of my ham friends in Nairobi for forwarding to Fleet Street. That was also unacceptable, answered the Swede.

Undeterred, I went ashore to try my luck at the local post office, irrespective of the fact that government spooks were to be found at every street corner in town. While the local postmaster was prepared to take my story as well as the Cable & Wireless card that went

Biafran MiniCon aviators. (Haglund photo)

with it for payment (sweetened by a $20 bill), my report was never sent. I shouldn't have been surprised because the country's military censors used blue pencils to impose a blanket ban on any news of Biafran air activity. Officially, they maintained, the MiniCons did not exist, even though I was told that London's *Lloyds List* covered the incident in some detail afterwards, as it does with all matters that pertain to international shipping.

ICRC airlift operations from a temporary strip in Calabar, 1968.(Photo CDC/ Dr Lyle Conrad)

7. THE MERCENARY COMPONENT

The A-26 Invader was a fast, twin-engined, light bomber and ground attack aircraft built by the Douglas Aircraft Company during World War II and which saw service in several Cold War conflicts. It attacked Nigerian army positions many times.

According to Michael Draper who wrote the authoritative *Shadows: Airlift and Airwar in Biafra and Nigeria 1967–1970*, Biafra acquired two of these aircraft by devious means, one of which had been operated for a number of years by the French Centre d'Essai en Vol (CEV) at Brétigny-sur-Orge where it was used for radar calibration. Though the aircraft's electrical bomb release mechanisms were still in place, they were designed to function with conventional bombs of a certain configuration and weight which meant that the planes needed a lot of work if they were going to be effective against the Nigerians. For a start, Biafran bombs were makeshift affairs, often fashioned from oil drums and gas cylinders, so they were in no way compatible with the relatively sophisticated systems in the Invader. Their pilots had no choice but to instruct their 'bombardiers' to physically hurl them out the bomb bay.

That also required some adaptation because the 'bombs' were made by a Biafran artificer, Willy Achukwe, whose former trade it was rumoured, lay in the manufacture of fireworks

Willy's bombs, recalls Draper, "were marvels of ingenuity and even included delayed

Rolf Steiner.

action devices." One of the mercenary pilots, Polish World War II fighter ace Jan Zumbach described one of his creations as having a base containing phosphorus suspended in an insulating liquid. A Bickford fuse ran from this compartment through a partition plugged with wax into a second stage and this compartment contained gunpowder. The third was crammed with scrap metal.

"Two big nails protruded from the base of the bomb. The impact of hitting the target or the ground drove the nails and pierced the first compartment. An insulating liquid was released from these punctures which allowed for air exposure and, in turn, set the phosphorus alight. Resultant heat melted the wax and the Bickford fuse detonated the gunpowder." All very complicated but it seemed to work, unless something went wrong. That appeared to have happened when Biafra's lone F-27 Fokker Friendship blew up over Lagos while attempting to bomb the Nigerian capital.

As for machine guns for the A-26, there were none available in Biafra, so Zumbach improvised after visiting the government armoury from which he was invited to take his pick of available equipment. He returned to the airfield with two antiquated army-issue, Czech-made machine guns. Biafran mechanics soon had the first one mounted in the nose of the Invader with the barrel protruding out front.

The hapless forward gunner was obliged to crouch in the dim recesses of the nose cone, without any view of the outside world and no voice communication with his pilot. Again, Biafran ingenuity came to the rescue. A length of cord was attached to the gunner's arm, the other end threaded through to the cockpit. Zumbach, equipped with a simple home-made gunsight, simply tugged once on the cord to instruct the gunner to start firing and twice to stop. A simple solution.

The second machine gun was rigged to fire through the open bomb bay.

Quite a number of mercenaries headed to Biafra once the war started and included soldiers of fortune from many European countries, South Africa, Rhodesia, Australia, Canada, and Britain as well as one or two Chinese Nung fighters. The Foreign Legion was quite well represented and there was even a CIA operative eager to get in a bit of action at company expense: experiencing the goings-on in the belea-guered territory must have been a lot better than propping up the bar at the Federal Hotel on Lagos's Victoria Island.

There was also 29 year-old Nick Bishop from Philadelphia who added Biafra to the notches on his gun-butt after he had served under Colonel Mike Hoare in the Congo. With him in this desperate West African enclave was British 'Major' C. C. Watson, a claymore mines specialist who went on to help fine-tune the appropri-ately dubbed 'Ojukwu Buckets' that car-ried enough explosives to incinerate an armoured car.

There were actually more mercenaries active with the Biafran forces than are given credit for, in part because Ojuwku was reluctant to admit that these 'guns for hire' who earned $1,700 a month upwards were a vital adjunct to his fighting

A Biafran mercenary, with a bandaged hand, poses outside his lodgings.

capability. Not that there were any 'big bucks' to be made by fighting freelance in this jungle country where you had as good a chance of going down with an unspecified tropical disease as being shot in a 'friendly fire' accident by one of your own men.

When I met Frederick Forsyth in Washington in an effort to help him complete research for his forthcoming book, *The Afghan*, we were able to discuss the mercenary role in Biafra at length. Being close to the Biafran leader, he had obviously been at hand when some of these things took place, which was clearly why he had such a remarkable insight to the way things developed in this peculiar West African environment. It also tells us why he was able to write *The Dogs of War*: many of the characters he met in that conflict featured under assumed names and disguises in the novel which became an enormously successful bestseller. In a sense, Forsyth was the ultimate 'fly on the wall', unobtrusive but always there when things happened. More salient, he was a good listener. As he said, there was no question that a good deal of what appeared in his original novel came from time he spent in Biafra reporting, first for the BBC and, after he had resigned, independently.

There was no question that mercenaries played an important role. It is also interesting that a steady flow of mercenary hopefuls continued to arrive in the embattled enclave even after Biafra suffered its first defeats, though only a handful stayed the distance. Some of the men were more resolute that others and dug their spurs in deep. One was an ex-Legionnaire by the name of Rolf Steiner and another was the powerfully built Marc Goosens, a Belgian national of Flemish origin. Goosens had gone to the Congo in 1964 as

Battle of Britain Polish hero Jan Zumbach in front of his B-26 Invader.

Belgium's senior military adviser with the rank of colonel, tasked with the role of assisting Mobuto's Armée Nationale Congolaise (ANC), though he was actually an agent working for Belgian military intelligence. Four years later, as a Biafran major, he was battling the Nigerian army and was killed during an attack on Onitsha. The entire episode was captured on film, including his men hauling his body back to their own lines so that he could buried with honour.

Both Goosens and Steiner played useful roles in this terrible internecine conflict, though the German eventually overstepped the bounds and was abruptly hustled out of the country. He refused to go, but ended up in restraints when they put him on board an aircraft headed for Libreville.

The 'mercs' were certainly a mixed bunch and included people like Major Taffy Williams, a South African, though ethnically Welsh. He turned thirty-four while serving in Biafra. *Time* magazine recorded at the time—October 25, 1968—that he was a veteran of Colonel Mike Hoare's 5 Commando in the Congo: "He thinks he is bulletproof. By now, so do the Federals, who have reported him dead at least five times ... Taffy came perilously close to being killed a few weeks ago when a round smashed into his binoculars. Short-tempered, he curses his black troops constantly, threatening to kill them if they don't obey orders. 'You rotten bastards!' he would roar, when things went wrong, or 'you bloody, treacherous morons!'"

Jan Zumbach, Polish mercenary, in the cockpit of his B-26.

Williams was initially assigned about a hundred Biafran fighters and managed to effectively counter the presence of two battalions of mercenaries from the Chad Republic who were serving with the Nigerian Federal Army for three months. The Muslim fighters were all armed with modern AK-47s, while his men fielded outdated World War II weapons.

Completing his first contract and having returned to Britain for a break, Williams went back to Biafra in July 1968 and was assigned to the 4th Commando Brigade led by Steiner. The French Foreign Legion veteran had under his command a force of about 3,000 men and was deployed to the region along the critically important Enugu–Onitsha road, without which, the enclave would been split in two.

In August 1968, Williams was drawn into one of the most critical battles of the conflict. At this point, he had about 1,000 soldiers under him carrying out counter-offensive actions against two battalion-sized enemy units attempting to cross the Imo river bridge. The fact that the Nigerian force had Soviet military advisers in its ranks did not go unnoticed. When Williams returned to the town of Aba for additional ammunition to continue the fight, he was told that there was none. The NAF by then become successful in blocking supplies into the beleaguered state and some of Williams's men had only two rounds left for their rifles. Many were forced to withdraw.

A clean-cut Taffy Williams in a carefully posed shot.

By the time hostilities in Biafra ended, Williams had made a name for himself among this elite band of freebooters. Having served two tours of duty with the Biafran army, he was recognized for consistent bravery under fire, rising to the rank of major. He was also the last white mercenary to leave the country as secession ended, by which time he had earned the warranted respect of those who served under him. In fact, Williams later told a South African colleague, they would have done anything for him, which made good sense because he always led from the front. It is also notable that Williams found his Biafran troops to be completely different from those who he had commanded in the Congo's southern province of Katanga: "I've seen a lot of Africans at war," he was quoted as saying. "But there is nobody to touch these people. Give me 10,000 Biafrans for six months, and we'll build an army that would be invincible on this continent. I've seen men die here who would have won the Victoria Cross in another context."

Another 'freebooter', the so-called 'Captain Paddy', was an Irishman who had spent twenty-two of his more than fifty years in Africa and arrived independently from South Africa as a master mechanic with one of the units. *Time* tells us that just before Port Harcourt fell, he scrounged up a convoy of trucks and 'liberated'—under fire —the entire workshop of the Shell-BP refinery there. When Aba finally had to be evacuated for lack of ammo, Paddy was one of the last men out, a machine gun in one hand, a demijohn of wine in the other.

Another of these illustrious Europeans who were fighting this 'black man's war' was Captain Armand Ianarelli, a former French paratrooper and veteran of Algeria. He sported

Nigerian aviators with Klootwyk (right) at Kano airport in the North.

The empty plate says it all at a Biafran refugee camp for orphans. (ICRC photo)

a Yul Brynner pate and fought valiantly, despite bazooka fragments in one hand, and quickly made a name for himself by taking his men behind enemy lines and creating havoc. By the time he departed the enclave, people were referring to him as 'Armand the Brave'. According to Forsyth, Armand was actually a Corsican from Paris "who later secured a more comfortable assignment as bodyguard to Madame Claude in Paris; she was then the world's most famous procuress of top-class call girls," he recalled.

Captain Alec—Alexander Gay, a former British paratrooper—was another of Forsyth's mercenary pals. He used to walk around with a Madsen sub-machine gun, an FN rifle and a shotgun "just in case I have to shoot my way out of this bloody place". Gay told one scribe that he believed in the "little people", who, he would say in all seriousness, "will unknowingly jam your machine guns and cause your rockets to misfire." He was wounded four times in the week before he left Biafra.

Others who left their mark in the rebel enclave was 'Commandant' Kochanowsky, a middle-aged Pole who had served with the Eighth Army in North Africa and then spent some years in the Foreign Legion. Then there was the unlikely named Johnny Korea, a West Indian who claimed to have come from Barbados and who ran a bar in Eastern Nigeria before the war.

Forsyth: "Meanwhile, a few more unlikely war dogs dribbled in, all of them volunteers. The mercenary group also included a few more South Africans and a Rhodesian explosives expert. We'd all get together evenings and after a few drinks Taffy Williams would tell us that we were all crazy to be there and that he was the only certifiably sane person in the group. What he didn't tell us was that he'd actually got the certificate to prove it after being released from a lunatic asylum at some stage in his obscure past."

I never did get around to asking him whether he used Taffy Williams as the basis for his character Carlo Shannon in *The Dogs of War*, but the similarities are striking. Freddie maintained contact with Williams after the war, as he did with both Steiner and Gay, but they lost touch after a while, even though he did help them financially when they were in need.

From the start of the military campaign, the Biafran leader cultivated ties with several groups of freelance aircraft operators, some from Europe, one or two from the United States and several from southern Africa, including Rhodesia's illustrious Jack Malloch.

By now, Ojukwu had secretly launched a fairly extensive build-up of arms, most of it arriving by air, but with quite large shipments channelled through Port Harcourt, the rebel state's principal port. Together with arms merchants from France, Holland, Germany and China—people like Malloch and Hank Wharton— Ojukwu worked hand-in-glove with several European governments including France, Portugal and Spain in a bid to provide his miniscule army just about all it needed, always at a price.

Paris, as we learned earlier on, was more than offhandedly interested in what was going on in Nigeria at the time. The war was not going well for the rebel state and the last thing the Quai d'Orsay wanted was to be exposed as being Biafra's ultimate lifeline. Supplying weapons was one thing—that could always be denied and security at Libreville was tight enough to keep the journalists at bay—and anyway, just about everybody was supplying one country or the other with arms. Manpower, in the shape of French 'volunteers', or mercenaries, was another matter. Were that to be put onto the world stage, there was no saying what the outcome would be. The result was that this activity was kept secret. So was the South African military role because Paris was picking up that tab.

By linking itself to Paris's subterfuge, South Africa got involved. The plan orchestrated by Jacques Foccart, the Elysée's shadowy *eminence grise* in charge of African affairs for President de Gaulle, was to try to help Pretoria out of the isolation that had resulted from its years of race-motivated policies. Soon after hostilities in the Congo ended, France persuaded South Africa to provide the secessionists with arms and ammunition, largely because French ammunition didn't fit 'British standard' Biafran weapons. Pretoria eventually provided Ojukwu with hundreds of tons of ordnance as well as a squad or two of Special Forces troops.

Contact had originally been made with the future president, P. W. Botha, who, at the time, was South Africa's defence minister. He delegated responsibility for the liaison to General Fritz Loots, the original founder of the country's Reconnaissance Commandos, or more colloquially, the 'Recces'. Coordinating developments in Libreville was Neels van Tonder, a brilliant South African army staff officer who was eventually to leave his imprint on the Angolan war.

Other South Africans who got involved included such luminaries as Major Jan Breytenbach, one of the finest unconventional counterinsurgency specialists fielded by the South African military (and surprisingly, brother of arch anti-apartheid activist

South African mercenary pilot and his Soviet MiG-17 flown in Biafran combat missions. (Ares Klootwyk)

Breyten Breytenbach). Breytenbach at the behest of General Loots actually created the original 'Recces', the Reconnaissance Commandos, and later regiments such as 32 Battalion, an Angolan army detachment that had defected en masse to South Africa where these Portuguese-speaking troops were incorporated into the national army.

There was also Chris Moorcroft, Alan Heard and another old hand, Paul Els, all of whom, in one way or another, became involved in Biafran operations. Els's role was in communications, based in Libreville, the Gabonese capital.

One of Breytenbach's key players was 'FC' van Zyl, who only just survived a bout of typhoid after he was flown out of Biafra and put into an ICU unit at the best hospital in Gabon. There, acknowledging that his life hung in the balance, one of the doctors stayed at his bedside for two days and nights, until it became clear that he was over the worst. Others were not so lucky.

Still more South Africans were linked to training and tactical issues. It suited the Pretoria regime to cause dissension in Africa, largely because of domestic problems back home and was all part of South Africa's continent-wide programme of destabilization.

A typical refugee hospital, 1968. (Photo CDC/ Dr Lyle Conrad)

There was also an operation planned to get one of South Africa's French-built Daphne class submarines to a position off Lagos harbour and send in underwater demolition teams to blow up Russian freighters then bringing in arms for the Federal offensive. Inexplicably, said South African navy admiral Woody Woodburne, with whom I discussed the matter, the raid was called off at the last moment, which was perhaps just as well. Indirectly, I was involved in that little caper. Working in Lagos at the time, I was discreetly approached by Captain 'Solly' Cramer, South Africa's naval attaché in London, to see whether I could lay my hands on a set of maps detailing everything in Lagos harbour, which included Apapa docks. I did—a wadge of them in large scale—and sent them through to Cramer by devious means. Then I received an urgent message from the captain warning me to stop everything because he'd been tipped off that Nigerian intelligence services were onto me.

8. THE AIR BRIDGE

The following is an extract from a flight report from one of the pilots who regularly flew into Biafra bringing aid, dated May 1969: "We spent one hour and four minutes waiting in the air over the Uli field ... made five aborted approaches. Nigerian bombers were harassing as usual, the landing lights came on too late or were turned off on final approach. The 'Intruder'—that is, the Federal bomber—released his first bomb when we were at the end of our final approach..."

Uli airfield—formerly part of a main road in eastern Nigeria—was bombed incessantly during the war but the damage was quickly repaired. Losses were not prodigious: in fact, considering the risks and the reality of what the Nigerians were doing to stymie the relief effort, they were actually quite modest.

This partial list, below, offers something of an insight: In November 1968, a Joint Church Aid DC-6 was damaged by a twenty-kilogram shrapnel bomb that exploded alongside the aircraft. Five people were killed and many injured, including the co-pilot Jan Erik Ohlsen and the pilot Captain Kjell Bäckström. Ohlsen was flown out by a Red Cross plane but Bäckström decided to try and do the impossible and take his damaged aircraft out. It had fifty-something shrapnel holes along one side and two of its engines were leaking oil. Despite his injuries, Bäckström succeeded in getting himself, his crew and his aircraft to Sao Tomé, where he was operated on at the local hospital by Portuguese surgeons. Three pieces of shrapnel were removed from his body.

Eight crew members of the Red Cross were killed in a crash in May 1969 in a cargo aircraft carrying relief baby food and which was shot down by a NAF fighter jet in June 1969. Prior to that, four men died when a German aircraft crashed in July 1968, shortly before a Joint Church Aid aircraft had gone down. On 7 December 1968, a German DC-7 crash-landed at Uli, killing four.

On 4 August 1969, a Canadian Canairelief Super Constellation went down, killing its crew of four. Five Americans died in an air crash on 26 September 1969. Thereafter, four additional aircraft were totally destroyed without loss of life and two more damaged beyond repair, all at Uli. In spite of these losses in crews and machines, the air relief programme was considered relatively enormous. One needs to look at the figures to appreciate this.

In Christian church-backed relief flights alone (never mind arms-runs which made up a sizeable tally each night) there were 7,350 freight flights into Biafra in the three years that war ravaged eastern Nigeria. In this time—taking all flights into consideration—almost a million tons of supplies, including arms, were flown into the beleaguered territory.

During the course of all operations into Biafra fifteen aircraft were lost and twenty crewmembers killed, the majority buried in a small cemetery adjacent to Uli airport, later, as mentioned, bulldozed by Federal forces.

Rhodesian Mike Gibson (left) at the controls of an aid flight into Biafra.

A mercenary stalwart from the Biafra epoch, Jim Townsend, was well known to this rather unusual society of irregular freelance aviators. Much liked both personally and for his technical expertise in keeping aircraft that should never have left the ground operational, he was helped in recording some of his experiences by another aviator of the period, the late Peter Petter-Bowyer who went on to distinguish himself in the Rhodesian war.

Townsend's stories are illuminating, especially where he explains how he managed to keep clapped-out, four-engined cargo planes airborne, some veterans of World War II and way past their 'use-by' dates. Or where he deals with issues related to landing or taking off from African jungle airstrips better suited for a Tiger Moth or a contemporary Cessna-152. He recalls starting to fly for Hank Wharton whose crews were all part-timers, spending time on relief flights into Africa when they could pull away from their regular airline jobs in the United States. The majority were pretty competent, but there was also a handful that was a bit rusty because they hadn't flown Constellations for a while.

Others found the stress of landing on a succession of Biafran airstrips that had been carved out of the jungle enormously engaging. This was often done in total darkness and sometimes in tropical thunderstorms that would roar across the African coastline, the aircrews coping with dismal visibility and high winds with no more than three or four metres of tarmac on either side of their main wheels on touchdown. To all of them,

Townsend said, whatever their background, Biafra flights were always a challenge. Others called it dangerous, and there were quite a few pilots who did only one trip in and out of Biafra and headed home.

Townsend again: "I was lucky in that I managed to team up with a former South African pilot, Captain Petrie from Johannesburg, who had been on some of the bigger Constellations—the L-1600 series. We formed a good team and flew together for about six months, which meant that we could trust each other's judgement without question. That is why, I am sure, we came away unscathed—most of the time—in spite of experiencing just about every type of emergency imaginable. As a consequence, I became somewhat proficient in what the guys would refer to as 'hairy' situations, something that stood me in good stead later during the course of my flying career in the United States."

Of the Hank Wharton set-up, said Townsend, crews were always paid in American dollars—cash-in-hand from the man himself and nothing as mundane as cheques. That worked fine for many of the operators, the majority of whom didn't have bank accounts. "The truth was, that because there was not a lot of trust, we wouldn't consider going on another trip until we'd got paid for the last one. Hank Wharton had a German girl friend called Ziggy living with him and seemed to run the financial side of things, together with a lot else besides."

The Constellations that Wharton had at Lisbon had mostly flown in Lufthansa's distinctive livery and initially all were in good shape. But although there was a skeleton

A Boeing C-97 Stratofreighter lifts off from São Tomé island at dusk to deliver goods to beleaguered Biafra.

crew of professional German mechanics at Lisbon airport, they did very little of what Townsend referred to as preventative maintenance. They undertook only the rectification of flight defects and, sometimes, a sporadic pre-flight.

Townsend's average trip, with variations, was from Lisbon to Portuguese Guinea (Guiné-Bissau) and on to Nigeria's Port Harcourt and Ihalia, a small but strategic town to the east of the great city of Onitsha on the Niger river in Biafra. That was followed by a return to the Portuguese island of São Tomé and thereafter they would usually make their way back to Lisbon.

Normal flight time was about thirty or so hours from start to finish. 'Full duty' time was approximately thirty-five hours and with normal time on the ground there was an hour between each leg. "After each one of these trips I would end up sleeping for at least twenty-four hours in order get back to the normal world, but if we flew two trips a week I'd be completely shattered. The saving grace was the money, which was excellent."

Of course, he added, there was no such thing as routine 'duty' or 'flight times': "We just kept going like automatons and once settled down into something that resembled a cruise pattern, we'd take turns trying to doze off. This kind of routine went on for several years, and in that time I did my share of experimentation and learned a lot about pushing limits, sometimes extraordinarily so. But I did get the best performances and range on these trips ... As an example, the return leg from São Tomé to Lisbon was a fourteen-hour flight (empty) and obviously fuel was critical. If we arrived back at Lisbon with, say 1,000 pounds [170 gallons], we'd be chuffed, because under normal circumstances we should still have had about 3,000 pounds in hand because the Constellations we were flying did not have the kind of tip tanks installed as with the longer range models."

It is worth noting, he declared, that during all his time flying as a mercenary out of Portugal for Hank Wharton, Townsend lost only three aircraft. One was due to landing-gear problems going into Lisbon, one to a wing fire on takeoff out of São Tomé and the third was in Portuguese Guinea because a bomb had been secreted on the aircraft but it detonated prematurely while the plane was still on the ground. It was sabotage, he reckoned, intended to blow the plane apart en route.

Wharton's people did lose a few other aircraft from landing mishaps at Nigeria's Port Harcourt and at Ihalia in Biafra, as well as one or two that simply disappeared, sometimes into the sea. 'We suspected that one or two his aircraft crashed into the mountains in the Cameroon and Bill Brown, another flight engineer from Rhodesia was killed during a night-time go-around at Ihalia. "With regard to mishaps, I still have grey hair and very short fingernails as a legacy from our Lisbon to Biafra days."

One of the most illustrious of these aviators was Fred Cuny, an American World War II, disaster-relief veteran who was involved in several international missions, including Biafra. He was interviewed in 1995 by the BBC who featured him in the *Timewatch* documentary 'Biafra: Fighting a War Without Guns'. It was rebroadcast by the United States PBS network and is featured here in abbreviated form:

BBC: Could you tell me how and when you became involved in the Nigerian civil war?

Cuny: Well, it was an accident. I'd just finished working on a big project in Dallas—in fact I'd been working on helping design some of the systems for the Dallas Fort Worth airport. I got a call one night from an old professor of mine from college and he confessed that he'd taken a paper I'd written about Nigeria and the prediction that it made about the likelihood of a civil war in Nigeria back in the early 1960s and he had published it. And as a result of that he had been approached by some foundations who were interested in looking at the Biafran war to see what could be done when the war was over about getting humanitarian aid in for reconstruction. I'd always been interested in reconstruction. It was something I'd wanted to do. And he called and said he felt that he should get me involved in this project. So I said, "OK, fine. The two of us will do it together" and—I liked the guy. He was actually quite good despite the fact that he was using my paper.

And so we went off to Nigeria. I arrived in Lagos. I went up to the Foreign Ministry—got a meeting through the good offices of the United States Embassy there—and went to

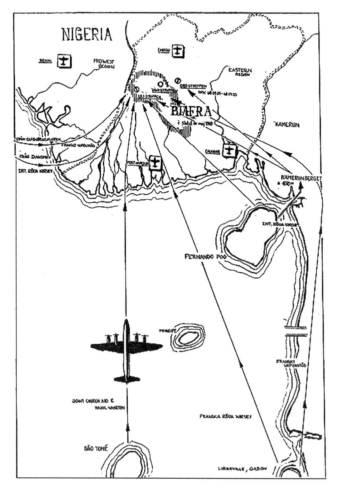

The São Tomé flight route into Biafra.

see the Minister of the Interior and said, "I'm from Texas and I'm here to study your war and tell you what you can do when it's over to get the humanitarian aid in here."

And the minister said, "Oh, that's interesting. Let's see your passport." And he thumbed through and got to the part where my visa was, ripped the visa out and said, "We don't want anything to do with these damned Biafrans and all you Americans and others that are helping them out and want you out of here in twenty-four hours" and threw the passport back. Then two guys came and escorted me to the airport, took all the money and put me on a plane.

So my partner in the study said, "That's it. I'm headed out of here" and he went back to the States. And I thought there might be some chance to salvage it. I didn't know anything about these organizations—the Red Cross or anybody else—so I went over and knocked on the door of the Red Cross and, "Hi, I'm from Texas and I'd like to look at your operations and see what we might be able to do when the war's over."

And the fellow who was in charge of the flight operations there said, "I haven't got time for this ... I've got a whole bunch of new airplanes coming in. I don't know how to use them. I don't know how to fly them. This whole thing is really crazy. We're having trouble with the Nigerians. My cargo systems are breaking down. Everything's a mess."

And I said, "Well, that's interesting. Cargo systems—I just worked on an airport, the world's largest airport in Texas and I know a little bit about that. And furthermore I'm a pilot. Maybe I can help you out."

He replied, "Well, you help me and I'll try and help you."

So I sat down and started working on the problems of integrating his new aircraft that were coming out and the first ones arrived and then I went out and helped check out with him and next thing I knew I was heavily involved in the airlift.

BBC: You worked as part of a large group of pilots flying into Biafra. Who were the pilots? Where did they come from?

Cuny: Oh, they were all sorts of people. Some of them were contract pilots from a Swiss company called Belair and they were recruited largely from the United States. The airplanes that we were flying at the time were the Boeing C-97 Stratofreighter which was a cargo version of the World War Two strategic bomber, the B-29.

The old Super Constellations were popular among aid crews going into Biafra.

The hulk of a Super Constellation rots away at São Tomé aiport.

So what we had to do was to find people who were qualified on the airplane or similar airplanes and get them qualified. So they recruited from some people who'd been in reserve units in the States and they got a number of Israelis that knew how to fly them and how to maintain them, which is even more important.

Some guys were mercenaries who couldn't find a job flying guns. Others were idealists. There was a real mixed bag of people. The fellow that I was closest to in my crew was there because he believed in the Biafran cause and he refused to take any money to fly. The chief pilot was a former Air America pilot. He'd been in and out of all sorts of scrapes in various places and a very colourful character. We had one guy who was a Baptist missionary who saw the Biafrans as some lost tribe of Israel that had to be salvaged—or saved. It was a real mixed bag. We actually used to call it the world's largest flying zoo.

But I think everybody there was dedicated to the mission and the more you got involved in the flying the more you began feeling something for the people and even the hardest nosed guys were always willing to run the risks of going in at night in these crazy places and delivering the goods because they felt very emotional about the need to try and keep people alive.

BBC: Could you describe to me how the airlift differed from the more conventional airlift of supplies?

Cuny: Well, first of all there was no coordination. We had many different aircraft that were going into the various airfields. The airfields are a misnomer. They were wide spots in the roads in a lot of cases. No traffic control to speak of. At one time we had a guy in a jeep with a hand-held radio that was coordinating all the traffic.

Most of the airfields in the latter stages of the war were under fire. The relief flights that were going in had been announced to the Nigerian authorities to try and gain them protection, but often the gun-runners would try and mask their flights by getting up underneath and flying close behind to get in. The airlift had a variety of different organizations. You had the International Committee of the Red Cross [ICRC] which was probably the best managed and operated airlift component. They had six of those huge C-97s.

You also had Inter Church Aid which was really the biggest private group that was there and what they did is they had first a variety of different aircraft. Some were old Constellations, others were LC-54s or the DC-4s, several DC-6s: a real mix of aircraft.

And the planes had different speeds. They had different capacities and with no schedule they'd arrive over different airfields at different times and sometimes at the same time and it was always hairy because if you get there when somebody else is on the ground you can't get in. Have to circle and there's always the danger of interception or being shot at by ground fire. So there were times when it was pretty chaotic.

Numerous times we tried to work out various arrangements and the ICRC who wanted to try and get permission to fly daylight flights, announced through a special corridor where they wouldn't be shot down. But the Nigerians kept denying them permission to fly and there were all sorts of problems with that.

(Cluny died in mysterious circumstances in Chechnya shortly afterwards, while trying to negotiate a ceasefire in that embattled Russian dependency. His body was never recovered.)

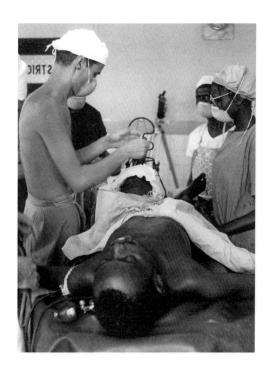

A wounded Biafran soldier being treated in a
bush hospital (ICRC photo)

9. FINAL RECKONING

"A great deal of subterfuge and intrigue enveloped British government involvement in the Nigerian conflict. It hardly helped that Whitehall was linked to Moscow in its bid to destroy Biafra."*

As a consequence of Colonel Ojukwu's actions to break with Lagos, the Biafrans were immediately classed as pariahs, especially once the prospect of an independent country started to loom large.

As one British civil servant phrased it in a London briefing, the easterners, with some notable exceptions, were a group of unprincipled rebels and it was clear that they were potentially damaging to British interests in Africa, Nigeria especially.

This was all off the record of course, because by then there was a fairly large eastern Nigerian community already resident in Britain, the majority extremely distressed by the murders of their people by northern Muslims, many of them relatives.

The argument along Whitehall's corridors of power was that if Ojukwu succeeded in tearing Nigeria apart, who then knew where next some African upstart would decide to go it alone. As it was, factional differences had surfaced in several countries: the Sudan, Uganda, Kenya (with the Luo and the Kikuyu tribal groups reticent to sit around the same table) and the African and Omani Arab communities in Tanzania's Zanzibar Island, which had experienced much bloodshed just five years before.

What had possibly irrevocably swung it for the U.K. to stand fast with Lagos was the fact that Ian Smith had unilaterally broken ties with the motherland and declared Rhodesia a sovereign state just a short while before. That country had governed itself since 1923 and the 1965 UDI came as something of disappointment to the British because so-called 'kith and kin' were responsible for the severance, regarded by London as reprehensible.

Nigerian people, unlike Rhodesians, shared no common heritage with Britain, which meant, in theory, that it would be that much easier to split the nation. Looking back, it was obviously Nigeria's immense oil resources that gave the Nigerians, the British and Lagos's newfound ally, Moscow, pause for thought.

It is interesting that shortly before this book went to print, a number of classified government files that related to the Biafran War were released in London in August 2017. A half century had passed since these events had taken place and they are now in the public domain. Some of the details that have emerged after all this time are mesmeric because they display very clear links between the government of Lieutenant-Colonel Yakubu Gowon and Whitehall. Others are damning, because of the cavalier approach by some British civil servants toward a crisis that, at that early stage, might have been halted

---

* Al J. Venter, *Biafra's War: A Tribal Conflict in Nigeria that Left a Million Dead.*

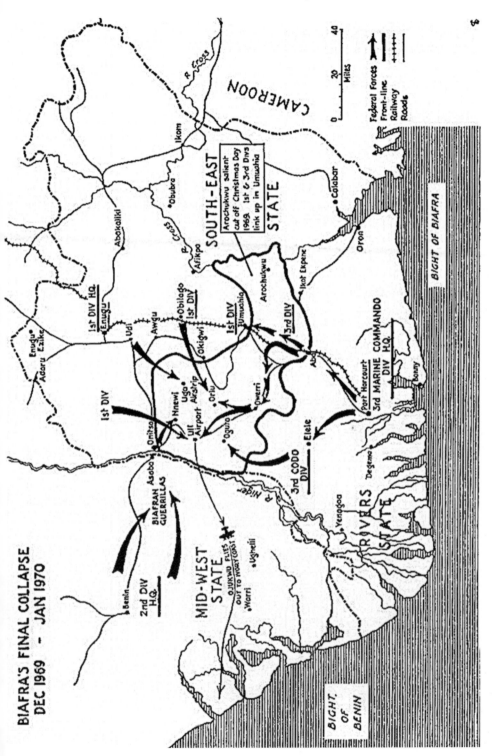

The final collapse.

had investment and financial interests not dominated the decision-making process. Comments made by George Thomas, Harold Wilson's Commonwealth Minister, are especially pernicious. Other would call it avarice. A heading of one of the earlier documents makes for clear purpose and quotes a spokesperson for the Foreign Office in a statement made a few days before the outbreak of war in West Africa: "Our direct interests are trade and investment, including an important stake by Shell/BP in the Eastern Region. There are nearly 20,000 British nationals in Nigeria, for whose welfare we are of course specially [sic] concerned."

It also declared that Shell-BP's investments amounted to around £200 million, with other British investment in Nigeria accounting for a further £90 million. The oil company was then partly owned by the British government and almost all the oil reserves lay under the ground in the Eastern Region. Commonwealth Minister George Thomas underscored all this when he wrote in August 1967: "The sole immediate British interest in Nigeria is that the Nigerian economy should be brought back to a condition in which our substantial trade and investment in the country can be further developed, and particularly so we can regain access to important oil installations."

He further outlined the primary reason why Britain was so keen to preserve Nigerian unity, noting that "our only direct interest in the maintenance of the federation is that Nigeria has been developed as an economic unit and any disruption of this would have adverse effects on trade and development". If Nigeria were to break up, he added,

Nigerian air power eventually cracked Biafran resolve. Here a village in the east takes a hit from the MiGs.

"We cannot expect that economic cooperation between the component parts of what was Nigeria, particularly between the East and the West, will necessarily enable development and trade to proceed at the same level as they would have done in a unified Nigeria. Nor can we now count on the Shell/BP oil concession being regained on the same terms as in the past if the East and the Mid-West assume full control of their own economies."

Ojukwu initially tried to get Shell-BP to pay royalties to his government rather than the Federal government. The oil companies, after giving the Biafrans a small token payment, eventually recanted and the Biafran leader responded by sequestering Shell's property and installations, forbidding the oil company to do any further business and ordering all its staff out.

A key British aim throughout the war was to secure the lifting of the blockade which Gowon imposed on the East and which halted not only all oil exports but any other movement as well, cargo and personnel.

In the run-up to Gowon's declaration of war, Britain had made it clear to the FMG that it completely supported Nigerian unity. George Thomas actually told the Nigerian high commissioner in London at the end of April 1967 that "the Federal government has our sympathy and our full support" but added that he hoped the use of force against the East could be avoided.

The Ilyushin-28 bomber nicknamed 'Genocide' at the Nigerian war museum in Umuahia.

On 28 May, having just declared a state of emergency, Gowon explicitly told Britain's defence attaché in Lagos that the FMG was likely to "mount an invasion from the north". Gowon asked whether Britain would provide fighter cover (aircraft) for the attack and naval support to reinforce the blockade of Eastern ports. The British representative replied that both were out of the question. Britain refused Nigerian requests to be militarily involved and urged Gowon to seek what was termed a 'peaceful' solution. However, in a conciliatory move, the Wilson government assured Gowon of British support for Nigerian unity at a time when military preparations were taking place. Very discreetly, London gave no indication that it might cut off or reduce arms supplies if a military campaign were launched.

The new high commissioner in Lagos, Sir David Hunt, wrote in a memo to London on 12 June 1967 that the "only way ... of preserving unity [sic] of Nigeria is to remove Ojukwu by force". He said that Ojukwu was committed to remaining the ruler of an independent state and that British interests lay firmly in supporting the FMG. In this regard it should be recalled that Frederick Forsyth had been in Nigeria for some time and had met with Sir David several times. His impressions were that the high commissioner regarded just about all black people—Ibos especially—with unconcealed disdain. More to the point, Sir David clearly displayed his colours by deprecating just about everything that the eastern leader said or did.

That approach obviously coloured the high commissioner's view of Colonel Gowon, who became a regular caller at Sir David's offices in Lagos. Long before going to war, Gowon—very much aware of the implications of what was happening in his country—began compiling a 'shopping list' of arms that his government wanted from Britain.

Ojukwu contemplates his future.

On 1 July 1967, he asked Britain for jet fighter and bomber aircraft, six fast boats and two dozen anti-aircraft guns.

The British responded by declaring that it wanted to "help the Federal Government in any way we can", however rejected supplying the aircraft, fearing that they would publicly demonstrate direct British intervention in the conflict; also rejected was supplying the boats. The British did however agree to sell anti-aircraft guns and to provide training courses to use them.

The deputy high commissioner in Enugu, Biafra's main city, noted that the supply of these anti-aircraft guns and their ammunition would be seen as British backing for the Federal Military Government and also that they were not entirely defensive weapons since "they could also take on an offensive role if mounted in an invasion fleet".

Nevertheless, Harold Wilson's media department was instructed to stress the "defensive nature of these weapons" when pressed, but generally to avoid publicity on their export from Britain.

Hunt added his bit to this imbroglio by stating that "it would be better to use civil aircraft" to deliver these guns and secure agreement from the Nigerians that "there would be no publicity" in supplying them.

Faced with Gowon's complaints about Britain not supplying more arms, Wilson agreed in mid-July 1967 to let the FMG have the fast patrol boats it had asked for. This was done in the knowledge that they would help Gowon's army maintain the blockade against Biafra. Wilson wrote to the Nigerian leader, saying that "we have demonstrated in many ways our support for your government as the legal authority in Nigeria and our refusal to recognize the secessionists".

He also said that Britain did "not intend to put any obstacle in the way" of orders for "reasonable quantities of military material of types similar to those you have obtained here in the past".

Gowon's riposte came back immediately: "I have taken note of your concurrence for the usual purchases of arms supplies to continue and will take advantage of what is available now and others when necessary."

A month later Biafran forces had made major gains against the FMG and had invaded the Mid-West region. Commonwealth minister George Thomas noted that "the chances of a clear-cut military decision being achieved by either side now look rather distant". Rather, "we are now faced with the probability of an escalating and increasingly disorderly war, with both sides shopping around for arms". In this situation, he raised the option of Britain launching a peace offensive and halting all arms supplies.

But this approach was rejected by Hunt in Lagos and others since it would cause "great resentment" on the part of the FMG against the British government and be regarded as what he termed "a hostile act". Instead, his government decided to continue the flow of arms and ammunition of types previously supplied by Britain but to continue to refuse supplies of "sophisticated equipment" like aircraft and tanks. That restriction did not hold for very long because soon afterwards new FV601 Saladin armoured cars were spotted being offloaded from British ships in Apapa docks. I was to discreetly take some photos of this development from one of the ships myself.

A gathering of starving Biafran children at the end of the war; most were dead inside a month.

A Biafran commentator subsequently made the comment that the decision to continue arms exports to the FMG was taken when it had already become clear in the behaviour of the Nigerian forces that any weapons supplied would be likely to be used against civilians. It was also when Commonwealth secretary-general Arnold Smith was making renewed attempts to push for peace negotiations, having been rebuffed by Gowon in a visit to Lagos early July 1967.

A word about the one weapon which arguably caused the most damage to Biafran forces in their defence of eastern Nigeria, the FV601 Saladin, a six-wheeled armoured car. Manufactured in the UK by Alvis from a 1954 design, it replaced the AEC armoured car in service with the British army from 1958 onward. The vehicle is listed with a weight (armed and fuelled) of eleven tonnes, with a 76mm low-pressure smoothbore cannon and a top speed of 72 kph, which was good for that period. Noted for its excellent performance in primitive conditions, the three-man Saladin found favour with a number of Third World armies, including several countries in the Middle East as well as Nigeria.

The tragedy for Biafra's Colonel Ojukwu is that his forces had absolutely nothing available with which to counter this weapon even though he tried hard to acquire French infantry fighting vehicles. Had he got them, it raises the question how to bring them in through what had become an extremely effective land and sea blockade. As for the Saladins, in the words of one British observer with the Nigerian army in an attack on Biafran defences near Onitsha, "they cut through Biafran defences like butter."

BIBLIOGRAPHY

Achuzia, Joseph, *Requiem Biafra* (Enugu, Nigeria, 1986)

Adebayo, Major-General Robert, *Onward Soldier Marches On* (Ibadan, Nigeria, 1998)

Adewusi, Richie, *Biafra: Lest We Forget* (Bloomington, Ind, 2011)

Alabi-Isama, Godwin, *The Tragedy of Victory: On-the-spot Account of the Nigeria-Biafra War in the Atlantic Theatre* (Ibadan, Nigeria, 2013)

Aneke, Luke Nnaemeka, *The Untold Story of the Nigeria-Biafra War* (London, UK, 2008)

Armand, Captain, *Biafra Vaincra* (Paris, France, 1969)

Baxter, Peter, *Biafra: The Nigerian Civil War 1967–1970* (Solihull, UK, 2014)

Boutet, Remy, *L'effroyable Guerre du Biafra* (Paris, France, 2004)

Cagnoni, Romano, *Il Mondo a Fuoco* (Rome, Italy, 2000)

Cervenka, Z., *The Nigerian Civil War* (Frankfurt, West Germany, 1971)

Clergerie, Jean-Louis, *La Crise du Biafra* (Paris, France, 1985)

Collis, Robert, *Nigeria in Conflict* (London, UK, 1970)

Cronjé, Suzanne, *The World and Nigeria* (London, UK, 1972)

Crowder, Michael, *The Story of Nigeria* (London, UK, 1978)

Draper, Michael & Forsyth, Frederick, *Shadows: Airlift and Airwar in Biafra and Nigeria 1967–1970* (Crowborough, UK, 1999)

Ebba, Obi, *Broken Back Axle: Unspeakable Events in Biafra* (Bloomington, Ind, 2010)

Efiong, Philip, *Nigeria and Biafra: My Story* (New York, NY, 2011)

—————, *The Caged Bird Sang no More: My Biafra Odyssey 1966–1970* (Solihull, UK, 2015)

Egbujor, Virginia, *As the Sky Darkened: The Untold Story of Biafra the Homeland* (Bloomington, Ind, 2014)

Elaigwu, J. Isawa, *Gowon: The Biography of a Soldier Statesman* (Ibadan, Nigeria, 1986)

Emefiena, Ezeani, *In Biafra Africa Died* (London, UK, 2012)

Forsyth, Frederick, *The Biafra Story* (London, UK, 1969)

—————, *The Biafra Story: The Making of an African Legend* (London, UK, 1983)

—————, *The Outsider: My Life in Intrigue* (London, UK, 2015)

Forsyth, Frederick & Byrne, Tony, *Airlift to Biafra: Breaching the Blockade* (New York, NY, 1997)

Gbulie, Ben, *Nigeria's Five Majors: Coup d'Etat of 1966* (Onitsha, Nigeria, 1981)

—————, *The Fall of Nigeria* (Enugu, Nigeria, 1989)

Gilles Caron, Bonneville, F., *La Mort au Biafra!* (Paris, France, 1967)

Gould, Michael, *The Biafran War: The Struggle for Modern Nigeria* (London, UK, 2012)

Graham-Douglas, Nabo, *Ojukwu's Rebellion and World Opinion* (London, UK, 1970)

Hunt, Sir David, *Memoirs Military and Diplomatic* (London, UK, 1990)

Ike, Chukwuemeka, *Sunset at Dawn* (Ibadan, Nigeria, 1976)

Ikpe, Samuel, *Red Belt: Biafra Rising* (London, UK, 2013)

Imoh, Chima, *Biafra: Conflicts, Principles, and Death of the General* (Houston, Tex, 2012)

Kirk-Greene, Anthony, *Crisis and Conflict in Nigeria* (Oxford, UK, 1975)

Koren, David L., *Far Away in the Sky: A Memoir of the Biafran Airlift* (Oakland, Calif, 2012)

Lewis, Stephen, *Journey to Biafra* (Ontario, Canada, 1968)

Mezu, Dr Sebastian Okechukwu, *Nigeria, Ojukwu, Azikiwe: Beyond the Rising Sun* (Baltimore, Md, 2012)

Nicholson, Mike, *A Measure of Danger: The Memoirs of Legendary War Correspondent Michael Nicholson* (Long Beach, Calif, 2014)

Niven, Rex, *The War of Nigerian Unity* (Ibadan, Nigeria, 1970)

Nkwocha, Dr Onyema, *The Republic of Biafra: Once Upon a Time—My Story of the Biafra-Nigerian Civil War* (Bloomington, Ind, 2012)

Nwanko, Arthur Agwuncha, *Nigeria: The Challenge of Biafra* (London, UK, 1972)

Odu P. J., *The Future that Vanished: A Biafra Story* (Bloomington, Ind, 2009)

Ogunsheye, F. Adetowun, *A Break in the Silence: Lt. Col. Adebukunola Victor Banjo* (Ibadan, Nigeria, 2001)

Okeke, Godfrey, *The Biafra-Nigeria War: A Human Tragedy* (Self-published, 1968)

Okotcha, E., *Blood on the Niger: The Untold Story of the Nigerian Civil War* (Port Harcourt, Nigeria, 1994)

Okpe, Captain August, *The Last Flight: A Pilot Remembers the Air Force and the Biafran Air Attacks* (Nigeria, 2011)

Ojukwu, C. Odumegwu, *Biafra: Random Thoughts of C. Odumegwu Ojukwu* (New York, 1969)

Oyeweso, Siyan, *Perspectives on the Nigerian Civil War* (Lagos, Nigeria, 1982)

Saro-Wiwa, Kenneth, *On Darkling Plain: An Account of the Nigerian Civil War* (Port Harcourt, Nigeria, 1989)

Schittly, Louis, *L'Homme qui Voulaitvoir la Guerre de Près: Médecin au Biafra, Vietnam, Afghanistan, Sud-Soudan* (Paris, France, 2011)

Sherman, John, *War Stories: A Memoir of Nigeria and Biafra* (Indianapolis, Ind, 2012)

Sidos, François-Xavier, *Les Soldatslibres: La Grandeaventure des Mercenaires* (Paris, France, 2008)

Siollun, Max, *Soldiers of Fortune: A History of Nigeria* (Abuja, Nigeria, 2013)

St Jorre, John de, *The Brothers' War: Biafra and Nigeria* (New York, NY, 1973)

Steiner, Rolf & Cox, S., *Last Adventurer: From Biafra to the Sudan* (Littlehampton, UK, 1978)

Stremlau, John, *The International Politics of the Nigerian Civil War* (Princeton, NJ, 1977)

Ugochukwu, Françoise, *Biafra, La Déchirure: Sur les Traces de la Guerre Civile Nigériane de 1967–1970* (l'Harmattan, Paris, France, 2009)

Umweni, Samuel, *888 Days in Biafra* (Lincoln, Nebraska, 2007)

Uwechuwe, Raph, *Reflections on the Nigerian Civil War: Facing the Future* (London, 2006)

Uzokwe, Alfred, *Surviving in Biafra: The Story of the Nigerian Civil War* ((Lincoln, Nebr, 2003)

Venter Al J., *Africa at War* (Old Greenwich, Conn, 1974)

——————, *Africa Today* (Johannesburg, South Africa, 1975)

——————, *Iran's Nuclear Option* (Philadelphia, PA, 2005)

——————, *War Dog: Fighting Other People's Wars* (Philadelphia, PA & Oxford, UK, 2006)

——————, *Barrel of a Gun: Misspent Moments in Combat* (Philadelphia, PA & Oxford, UK, 2010)

——————, *War Stories by Al Venter and Friends* (Pretoria, South Africa, 2011)

——————, *African Stories by Al Venter and Friends* (Pretoria, South Africa, 2013)

——————, *Mercenaries: Putting the World to Rights with Hired Guns* (Philadelphia, PA & Oxford, UK, 2014)

——————, *Biafra's War 1967-1970, A Tribal Conflict that Left a Million Dead* (Solihull, UK, 2018)

Waugh, Auberon and Cronjé, Suzanne, *Biafra: Britain's Shame* (London, UK, 1969)

Whiteman, Kaye, *A Last Look at Biafra* (London, UK, 1970)

Index

Al J. Venter is a specialist military writer who has had over fifty books published. He started his career with *International Defence Review*, covering military developments in the Middle East and Africa. He has been writing on insurgencies across the globe for half a century, involved with Jane's Information Group for more than thirty years. He was a stringer for the BBC, NBC News, as well as London's *Daily Express* and *Sunday Express*. He branched into television work in the early 1980s, producing more than a hundred documentaries, including *Africa's Killing Fields*, on the Ugandan civil war, and *AIDS: The African Connection*, which was nominated for a Pink Magnolia Award. His last major book, *Portugal's Guerrilla Wars in Africa*, was nominated for New York's Arthur Goodzeit military history book award. Venter writes extensively for several Pen & Sword military history series including 'Cold War 1945–1991' and 'A History of Terror'.

OTHER SERIES TITLES BY AL. J. VENTER

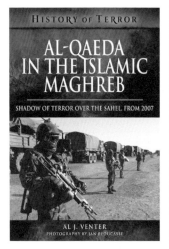

HISTORY OF TERROR

AL-QAEDA IN THE ISLAMIC MAGHREB

SHADOW OF TERROR OVER THE SAHEL, FROM 2007

AL J. VENTER
PHOTOGRAPHY BY IAN PEDUCASSE

COLD WAR 1945–1991

ANGOLAN WAR OF LIBERATION

COLONIAL–COMMUNIST CLASH, 1961–1974

AL J VENTER

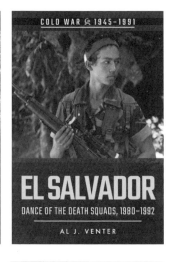

COLD WAR 1945–1991

EL SALVADOR

DANCE OF THE DEATH SQUADS, 1980–1992

AL J. VENTER

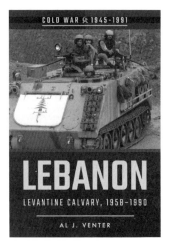

COLD WAR 1945–1991

LEBANON

LEVANTINE CALVARY, 1958–1990

AL J. VENTER

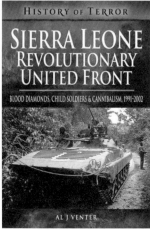

HISTORY OF TERROR

SIERRA LEONE REVOLUTIONARY UNITED FRONT

BLOOD DIAMONDS, CHILD SOLDIERS & CANNIBALISM, 1991–2002

AL J VENTER

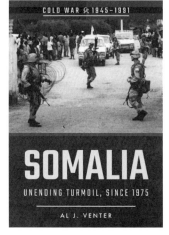

COLD WAR 1945–1991

SOMALIA

UNENDING TURMOIL, SINCE 1975

AL J. VENTER